TRIATHLON

A COMPLETE GUIDE FOR TRAINING AND RACING

to my parents

TRIATHLON

A COMPLETE GUIDE FOR TRAINING AND RACING

DR JOHN HELLEMANS
Foreword by Erin Baker

REED

acknowledgements

I would like to thank my wife, Ien, and my two daughters, Fleur and Saar, for putting up with my indulgence in the sport which I love. My thanks also go to Erin for her input into the chapters on "Racing" and "Women in triathlon", and Lifespan Smokefree, the Health Sponsorship Council of New Zealand, for its support. A special mention of John Durning's assistance in giving me deadlines, with a smile, as he knew I would miss them all. There are many others, too numerous to name, who I would also like to thank, for the influences they have had on my career and work associated with putting together this book.

National Library of New Zealand
Cataloguing-in-Publication data

Hellemans, John
    Triathlon: a complete guide for training and racing / John Hellemans ; foreword by Erin Baker. Rev. ed. Auckland [N.Z.] : Reed, 1993.
      1 v.
    First ed. published in 1988 as: Triathlon: the winning edge / Erin Baker, John Hellemans, Auckland, N.Z.: Heinemann Reed.
    ISBN 0-7900-0288-4
    1. Triathlon--Training. I. Baker, Erin. Triathlon: the winning edge. II. Title
      796.407   zbn 92-101380

Published by Reed Books, a division of Reed Publishing (N.Z.) Ltd, 39 Rawene Road, Birkenhead, Auckland.

Associated companies, branches and representatives throughout the world.

ISBN 0-7900-0288-4

© John Hellemans, John Durning 1993
Designed by Peet Lichtenberg
Formatted by the Postgraduate Printery,
Christchurch School of Medicine, New Zealand

Cover photographs of Erin Christie, Ken Glah and Ironman swimmers by Niels Schipper

First published as *Triathlon: The Winning Edge*, 1988
Revised edition 1993
Reprinted 1995, 1997

foreword

I first met John Hellemans when I was about 18 and running for the New Brighton Athletic Club in my home town of Christchurch, New Zealand. He was in the "A" relay team for road and cross country and because this team always won the prestigious national road relay title, I was impressed.

It was actually in Australia where we met again, this time at a triathlon - the Queensland Championships. There were 400 Australians in the race, some very well performed and world-ranked Americans, and a couple of "unknown" New Zealanders.

John won the men's race and I the women's. This was really the start of us as a "team". John convinced me to return to New Zealand to train and become a full-time triathlete.

From that day he has been my motivator, the brains behind the scenes, and I certainly could not have come this far without his ever-present expert knowledge and guidance.

At times he has appeared very stern and hard, he even made me cry on an occasion or two, but always his training technique and work ethic have proven to be the high road.

My only regret in regards to John is that the sport did not develop in New Zealand five years earlier as I believe John Hellemans would have been No. 5 of the "Big Four".

Read and learn, you could not get better advice on the sport of triathlon anywhere in the world.

Erin Baker

contents

introduction

What drives people to take part in one of the most gruelling contests ever devised where the body's physical limits are often tested, and sometimes breached, and the extremes of mental endurance are completely uncovered? Is it because of a rekindling of the "frontier spirit" - of training hard and playing hard - or is it the attraction of the unknown, that makes people become embroiled in the mystique of triathlons?

This extraordinary sport means different things to different people, from finishing an event, bettering a time, gaining a place, or winning. The common factor is that it offers competitive enjoyment. But, to ensure that the maximum enjoyment and a feeling of achievement is attained, certain guidelines must be followed.

Triathlons mean different things to different people - from winning the race to just finishing.

This is the aim of *Triathlon - a complete guide for training and racing*, to give athletes a thorough understanding of how the body responds, adapts, recovers and regulates, when exposed to endurance sport. Without this basic understanding training eventually lacks direction and discipline and much valuable time can be wasted on "garbage" miles.

Except for the professional triathlete, most of us fit our training schedules around jobs, family and other interests. Time wasted on "garbage" training is time that could easily be spent in other pursuits. Quality is the essence.

Why waste time on exercise that is not going to be beneficial to your ultimate performance? There is nothing more disheartening than spending long hours training and then seeing your performance level dropping instead of surging ahead. The successful completion of a triathlon event is only as effective as the preparation time invested in proper training, which should be approached systematically and scientifically with attention given to both the obvious and minor aspects related to the event.

In the years since the first triathlon in San Diego in the mid 1970s, the sport has grown dramatically internationally. The nature of the event, with three different pursuits making up one entity, has neutralised the domination of elite competitors. The advantage of an individual athlete being one of the fastest swimmers, cyclists or runners, can often be cancelled out over the other two disciplines. This is why the above-average all-round athletes perform so well in triathlons. It is one sport where they can excel, even against the very best.

John Hellemans and his protege Erin Baker are two athletes who found their niche in the multi-discipline event.

The triathlon has given Hellemans an extra decade of competitive sport. He had been a successful swimmer in his native country, the Netherlands, in the 1970s and also played competitive water polo. After finishing his medical degree he emigrated to New Zealand in 1978 and settled in Blenheim. Water polo was not played in that area so he developed an interest in running. A year later he moved to Christchurch and continued his running career, winning several road races, especially those where hills were involved. Triathlons were only beginning to gain prominence in New Zealand in the early 1980s and with his running and swimming background, and the fact that "every Dutchman can ride a bike", he was drawn into the New Zealand Triathlon Championships in Auckland in 1982, an event he won by four minutes, much to his surprise and the surprise of many.

This revitalised his appetite for competitive sport and the three-discipline nature of the triathlon became "his" sport, both from a competitive point of view and also from a medical and health aspect. Not only was there the fascination of competing in a complex new sport, but the different demands required in training, held an aura all of their own. Trying to fit this new sport around a young family and medical practice added another dimension. His desire to put family and work above triathlons meant Hellemans did not have an abundance of time in which to train so what time he had, had to be used to the fullest. It had to be of the highest quality to

When the gun goes, the
bullshit stops.

get the maximum benefit from the minimum duration. Saturday was the one day he
had time to put in the necessary duration work.

One of the highlights of his career was in 1984 when he won the Queensland
Championships in Australia. The winner of the women's event was an unknown by
the name of Erin Baker and although the pair had run for the same club in
Christchurch several years before, these championships were the first time they
had sat together and discussed triathlons and training techniques.

Swimming and running were also part of the Baker background. Erin had
succeeded at age-group levels and provincial championships in both sports, and
while living in Sydney, Australia, in the early 1980s, had to cycle 40 km to work
because she was without a car. This added the third discipline to the two learned
when younger.

One of Baker's greatest attributes is her competitive instinct - her will to win, to
discipline her mind to one thing. She entered a few triathlons around Sydney
without knowing too much about the requirements of training or anything else and
was successful. Those successes took her to Queensland in 1984, her meeting
with Hellemans and her subsequent decision to move back to Christchurch to train
under Hellemans' guidance, and to become a full-time triathlete.

The compatibility and success of the partnership was shown shortly after when
Baker demolished a world class field at the Tooheys Great Lakes Triathlon in
Australia in April 1985, less than six months after coming under Hellemans' tuition.
With several people having to pull out of the event because of the cold, she
became the first woman to break 10 hours for a long distance event with her time
of 9 hrs 55 mins - 40 minutes in front of second (Patricia Puntous) and an hour
ahead of third (Sylvianne Puntous). She further established her credentials, and
those of her coach, later that same year with an emphatic victory in the World
Championships in Nice.

Since then Baker, guided by the techniques and philosophies of Hellemans, has been the single most dominant figure in women's triathlons with world titles in all distances including two Hawaii Ironman events (also twice runner up), plus the World Duathlon title.

As triathletes become faster and better skilled, they are thirsting for knowledge - knowledge of how their bodies work, and how different training regimes and diet affect training and racing and how a disciplined mind will allow them to focus on that single, optimum performance.

It is to athletes like John Hellemans, who have competed successfully with the best in the world (often out of season for the Southern Hemisphere triathlete) and who also have the specialised medical knowledge, that they are turning for guidance.

He has that knowledge and he now shares it with you.

John Durning

1

basic guidelines

Enjoyment and satisfaction are the two key ingredients to be gained from triathlon training and these can only be achieved by keeping to the basic principles of training for endurance events. Awareness of how to implement an appropriate training programme will dramatically reduce the risk of injury and over training. This is essential for improving performance.

The specific challenge of triathlon training is to blend three individual sports together to produce a peak performance in these disciplines on the day of the race. To achieve this, an insight into training frequency, duration and intensity is required, together with knowledge of different training methods. There is a tremendous difference in the levels and skills of individual athletes in the three disciplines. The amount of time available for training also varies greatly. This means that training programmes should be adapted towards the needs of individual triathletes more than in any other sport and the triathlete has to be prepared to take responsibility for their own schedules. But, at all times, they must abide by the principles of triathlon training.

Some of the following information is based on science, but most of it on experience, intuition and common sense.

warming up

Always start your training session with a proper warm up. A warm up will increase the circulation to the working muscles. This will increase the temperature which will enhance muscle performance. It is not necessary to do a time-consuming set of stretching and flexibility exercises. Depending on which discipline you have in mind, 10-15 minutes of easy swimming, cycling or running is sufficient. More specific stretching and flexibility exercises are optional and can best be done after the warm up or after the workout when the muscles are warm so there is less risk of injury. Remember, the warm up is not only a physical preparation, but also a mental one.

At this stage, you plan the training session in more detail depending on your state of fitness and the way you feel. After you have done that then concentrate on the task ahead, knowing that control is a crucial part of every training session. This mental concentration is more important during a hard workout than for an easy one. It is a misconception that warm weather requires no warm up or a shorter warm up. A warm up needs to be specific depending on the rest of the training session. When the training session contains shorter, faster repetitions the warm up should also contain some controlled speed work.

listen to your body

Relate your workload to the condition you are in at the time and the way you feel. In your training programme, allow for flexibility so alterations can be made. This requires discipline, but if applied properly, optimum control will be the result. The more control there is, the less likely things will go wrong.

Do not overdo it. In time this can produce injuries and persistent tiredness. Be prepared to adjust your programme if this happens. Irritability, difficulty in sleeping and fluctuating weight are all indications of too much training.

quality versus quantity

There is increasing evidence that the quality of a training programme is more important than the quantity. Many triathletes tend to prolong their workout rather than increase the tempo or workload when they get fitter. Not all workouts, however, can be done at high intensity. The secret is to balance all hard and easy sessions in a way which will result in optimum conditioning. The hard sessions will be done at sub-maximum and close to maximum intensity, either as time trials or interval training. The intensity will depend on the level of fitness at the time.

goalsetting

Set yourself realistic short term and long term goals, not only in racing, but also in training. Make sure you can follow your training programme without having to push too hard. Allow also for other (family and work) commitments. Be realistic about the improvement you can expect over a period of time and be aware of your limits to prevent too many disappointments. Remember that it will take at least five or six years before you reach your potential.

On the other hand, do not underestimate your own ability. This is especially the case for women triathletes.

train gradually

Increase the intensity and duration of your training schedule only by small weekly increments. The most common cause of injuries is "too much, too fast, too soon". Increase mileage by no more than ten percent a week while closely relating any increase in fitness to subsequent increases in intensity.

For novice triathletes initial easy workloads should be attempted on alternate days for the first six weeks so as to acquire a good base in a safe way. A good basic fitness can be acquired in 2-3 months, depending on previous exercise experience. To get into race shape, a well conditioned, experienced triathlete will require another 6-8 weeks of more specific triathlon training.

self-motivation

Commitment, dedication, determination and motivation are crucial elements in properly executing the often complicated and extensive training programmes of triathletes. Continuous self-motivation is needed more than in any other sport. Even for the recreational triathlete, conditioning in three different sports will involve some degree of discipline.

For the serious triathlete it is a way of life, the only way to cope with the relatively large amount of training required. But there is also a danger that too much commitment will cause loss of enjoyment. Loss of interest and enjoyment is one of the first signs of overtraining.

specialisation

If you take triathlons seriously, then all of your sporting activities should be aimed towards your sport - the triathlon. If you want to be competitive, you will never achieve your maximum performance if you take part in other sports during the triathlon season. This will not only upset your training routine, but it will increase the risk of injury.

Balancing the three sports is difficult enough. This equilibrium can be upset easily by taking part in other physical activities, even at a social level. This is one of the sacrifices the more serious triathletes have to make.

recovery

Recovery should be an integral part of the training programme of endurance athletes. Monitoring the relationship between "effort" and "recovery" is of great importance, especially as the training load increases. In triathlon training it is hard enough to find time for 2-3 disciplines in the one day which means that time for recovery is often sacrificed.

The solution is to incorporate recovery training workouts in which you recover while you train. Lack of recovery can be a significant limiting factor in improvement even if you follow the most brilliant training programme. This includes 9-10 hours sleep a night during a period of heavy training. Additional sleep during the day may be necessary in preparation for a long-distance event when an average of 5-8 hours of training is required for the serious triathlete.

continuity

Try to make exercise a daily routine, not only during the season but at all other times, although still allowing for one or two rest days a week. The intensity and duration of a workout can vary greatly depending on the time of the year, experience and expectations. Too much conditioning is lost if there is a period of no exercise at all. This loss makes a comeback much harder to achieve.

The triathlon has the advantage in that most injuries will still allow you to train in at least one of the three disciplines. Rather than rest, make the best of the time and work on improving that particular discipline.

technique

The importance of proper technique is often underestimated, especially in cycling and swimming. Too many triathletes still think that poor technique can be compensated for by an increase in mileage and effort. This is not so. Special sessions on technique are never wasted.

Technique requires constant attention, especially when the workload has been increased. Fatigue can spoil a good technique and loss of technique results ultimately in a poor performance. A knowledgeable observer can be of tremendous help in recognising a faulty technique. There are few athletes who can see and correct their own faults.

When out with other athletes make use of them and ask for comments on your style. It pays also to join a swimming, cycling and/or running club so you can train under the guidance of skilled coaches. Attention to technique is the only way to make dramatic improvements, especially in your weakest discipline.

responsibility

The biggest mistake is to mimic the training programme used by an elite triathlete thinking that it will enable you to repeat their performance. To maximise your own potential you have to be willing to experiment with your training. Every individual is unique and has a different constitution, level of skill, training ability and psychological makeup. This means that you have to find out for yourself what type of approach and what type of training best suits you. A knowledge of basic principles of training and examples of training programmes based on these principles can be used as a guide, but the ultimate responsibility for an individual's training programme lies with the triathlete.

2

muscles and their support organs

Physical exercise is directly related to the working muscles. Different organs in
the body are responsible for supplying the muscles with oxygen and fuel
(nutrients). Others assist with the elimination of waste products. Some of the most
important organs which assist the working muscles are: the circulation, lungs,
heart, liver, skin, kidneys, gut, and the hormonal and central nervous systems.

the muscles

Every sporting activity depends on the speed, strength, power and efficiency of the
muscle action. The co-ordination of a single muscle action with other muscle
groups is controlled by the central nervous system. Muscles are built of long cells
called muscle fibres. In the fibres are proteins (actine and myosine) which contract
and make movement possible. The main energy for muscle contraction during
endurance exercise is delivered by the mitochondria, which are the aerobic energy
stations of the muscle cells.

Not all muscle fibres are the same. Type 1 fibres are also called the aerobic, red,
or slow twitch fibres. Slow twitch fibres generate energy in the presence of
oxygen, have a high number of mitochondria and a good blood supply. Endurance
athletes usually have a high proportion of slow twitch fibres, up to 80 percent.
Slow twitch fibres use glycogen and fat as fuel.

Type 2 fibres are also called the anaerobic, white, or fast twitch fibres. The fast
twitch muscle fibres are capable of producing fast energy without the help of
oxygen. They have fewer mitochondria (anaerobic energy production takes place
in the cell fluid). Fast twitch muscle fibres are important in activities that require
sprinting and jumping. Sprinters average approximately 60 percent of fast twitch
fibres and 40 percent of slow twitch fibres. Fast twitch fibres can only use
glycogen as fuel. Some races have a genetic tendency towards more high twitch
or slow twitch fibres. American Blacks, for example, have a higher percentage of
fast twitch fibres which explains their superiority in sprinting and jumping events

and their absence in endurance events.

Regular aerobic training will do two things. It will increase the size of the slow twitch fibres and it will change some fast twitch fibres into slow twitch fibres over a period of time.

the circulation

The blood transports oxygen from the lungs and nutrients from the gut to the working muscle. Blood consists of plasma and blood cells. The nutrients are transported in the plasma and the oxygen is transported in the red blood cells. The plasma is also responsible for the transport of heat generated by the muscles, away from the muscles to the skin. There are two different blood cells, red and white. The red blood cells consist of haemoglobin, which binds oxygen and carbon dioxide, and gives the blood its red colour. One of the building stones of haemoglobin is iron. The white blood cells act as defence barriers against intruders like bacteria and viruses and when there is tissue damage they "clean up" the damaged area.

the lungs

The lungs are responsible for the exchange of the gases oxygen and carbon dioxide. The lungs branch out into smaller pipes and finally to microscopic lung vesicles where the exchange between O_2 and CO_2 takes place. CO_2 is a byproduct of the aerobic energy metabolism in the muscle cell. The blood circulation to the lungs contains plenty of CO_2 and little O_2. CO_2 is expelled into the lungs to be expired. The O_2, being sucked into the vesicles with inspiration, is absorbed by the circulation and bonded for its transport to the red blood cells. In rest we breathe 12-15 times per minute, replacing approximately six litres of air. During intense exercise this can increase to 30-60 breaths per minute replacing 100-200 litres of air.

the heart

The heart should be seen as a pump. It consists mostly of muscle and has its own electrical pacemaker which is responsible for regular contractions of approximately 60-70 beats per minute. In rest, the heart pumps approximately five litres of blood per minute, while during intense exercise this can increase to 30-40 litres per minute. This is achieved through a combination of an increased heart rate and heart volume.

In trained athletes the resting heart rate can lower from 60-70 beats per minute to 40-50 or even lower. This is because training causes an increase in the size of the heart which can then pump more blood per contraction.

The maximum heart rate is approximately 180 to 200, but this can be higher in younger persons. With age, the maximum heart rate usually drops significantly. There are, however, individual differences in maximal heart rate. Maximal heart rate does not have a relationship to fitness or performance, contrary to popular belief. The resting heart rate has. There is an inverse relationship between the resting heart rate and the level of aerobic fitness. Monitoring of the resting heart rate can assist in the monitoring of fitness. This can be applied in practice when training seriously for endurance events. Variations in resting heart rate, especially an increase of 6-10 beats, can signify illness or overtraining.

the liver

The liver's main function is to store carbohydrate which is slowly released into the blood stream as blood sugar. The liver plays an important role in keeping the blood sugar level constant while it also assists in breaking down nutrients absorbed by the gut, including alcohol and drugs. The liver has many other functions which are not directly related to exercise.

the skin

The skin is the body's protective shield. It prevents dehydration and acts as a barrier against bugs and other intruders. The skin has many sweat glands which assist with the temperature regulation of the body. If the production of heat, produced by the energy metabolism, is greater than can be conducted through the skin, the sweat glands will come into action. Through elimination of the sweat further heat is then dissipated.

the kidneys

The kidneys excrete excessive fluids and salts as well as other substances. In endurance exercise the kidneys are often working very hard to preserve the fluid and electrolyte balance. At the end stage of dehydration the kidneys can shut down completely which is a life threatening event.

the gut

The food we eat and drink is broken down in the gut and absorbed into the blood stream. Digestion is aided by the functions of the pancreas and liver which excrete substances in the gut that assist digestion. During intense exercise the blood supply to the gut can be compromised as the blood is shunted away to the working muscles. This can hamper digestion and irritate the gut. Gut problems during intense endurance exercise are common.

the hormonal system

The hormonal system acts as a messenger. Hormones are produced by special organs and excreted into the blood for transport to their target organs. The action of the hormones is either to activate or suppress the function of their target organ. The central nervous system is directly responsible for co-ordination and action of the different muscle groups involved in exercise. It can stimulate, inhibit and alter the function of the muscle. By training on muscle functions we also train the central nervous system to respond appropriately to exercise.

the central nervous system

The central nervous system (the brain and spinal cord) co-ordinate the functions of the different organs. The organs are connected with the central nervous system through the nerves which carry messages by electrical conduction. The central nervous system also regulates most of the hormone producing organs.

Ex-All Black Murray Davie lost 18 kg in the process of becoming a triathlete.

3

energy systems

the three energy systems

Energy in the working muscle cell is derived from ATP (adenosine tri phosphate). Energy for muscle contraction will be released when ATP is broken down to ADP (adenosine di phosphate) and a phosphate molecule. There is a limited amount of ATP available in the muscle cell. ATP can be regenerated by the rebuilding of the single phosphate molecule onto ATP. To ensure ongoing availability of energy for muscle contraction, ATP needs to be regenerated continuously.

Three different energy systems which are capable of resynthesising ADP plus P into ATP have been identified in the body. The three systems are the fast acting anaerobic alactic system, the anaerobic lactic system and the aerobic energy system (Fig. 1,2,3).

The anaerobic alactic system can provide immediate energy. It uses phosphagens stored in the muscle cell as its fuel. As there are very limited amounts of phosphagens available, the system runs out quickly (approximately 10 seconds). The anaerobic alactic system is mainly used in quick bursts of high intensity exercise, e.g. at the start of a triathlon or when sprinting. This system does not require oxygen and produces no lactic acid, hence the name anaerobic/alactic.

The anaerobic lactic system comes into play just before the anaerobic alactic system runs out. It uses carbohydrates exclusively as its fuel. This system also does not require oxygen, but it produces lactic acid and protons as byproducts. The anaerobic lactic system provides the chief source of energy for activities lasting between ten seconds and two minutes, when there is a shortage or absolute lack of oxygen. This system is used during triathlons at the start and at times during the event, for example when accelerating and hill climbing.

The aerobic energy system comes into play approximately two minutes into exercise and is dependent on the availability of oxygen. It uses fats and carbohydrates and certain portions of the protein chain called amino acids as its fuel. The aerobic energy system becomes the main energy source in events lasting more than three minutes, so in the triathlon it becomes by far the main provider of ATP and, therefore, energy.

Fig. 1

The breakdown and rebuilding process of ATP.

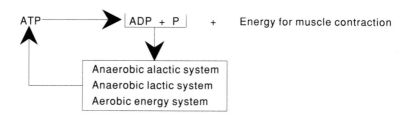

The aerobic energy system, although slow in production of energy compared with the anaerobic systems, is tremendously efficient. It produces 12-18 times as much ATP from one molecule of glucose as the anaerobic lactic system. The end products of the aerobic system are plenty of energy, water (which can be used in other areas of metabolism) and carbon dioxide, which is released into the atmosphere by the lungs.

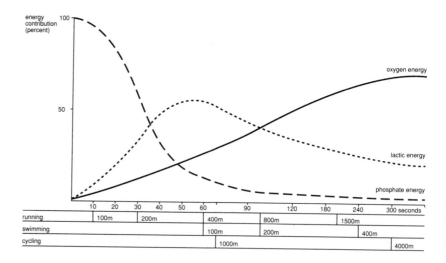

Fig. 2

Represents the energy contribution of the different energy systems over exercise time.

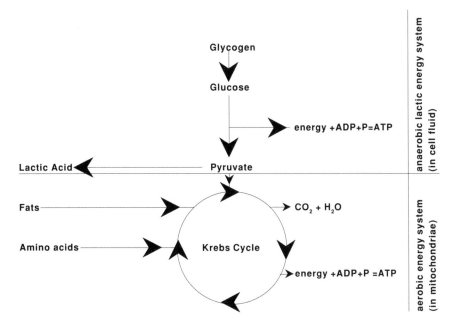

Fig. 3

A simplified outline of the many steps involved in anaerobic and aerobic energy systems. The Krebs Cycle applies to the steps involved in the aerobic breakdown of glycogen.

the lactate turn point (the anaerobic threshold)

The lactate turn point is the exercise intensity at which lactate concentrations rise rapidly. This coincides with the point where the oxygen supply to the muscle cell is unable to keep up with the demand.

The mechanism behind the lactate turn point is not totally clear. Initially it was thought that lactate was only produced during high intensity exercise, when the oxygen supply could not meet the oxygen demands of the muscle cell. However, a more current theory is that lactate is continuously produced and consumed in the muscle cell in rest, as well as during exercise. At low intensity exercise most lactate produced by the muscle cell will be locally consumed and, therefore, does not result in a noticeable increase in blood lactate concentration.

The higher the exercise intensity, the greater the contribution of carbohydrate to the energy metabolism, especially when the anaerobic pathways are also being engaged. This results in an accompanying increase in pyruvate and lactate production. When lactate production exceeds the local rate of lactate consumption, the lactate turn point is reached.

Until recently, lactic acid has been considered a waste product directly responsible for muscle soreness related to high intensity exercise. However, it appears that lactate in fact is an important metabolic fuel. Firstly, it can be metabolised within the muscle cell where it is produced. Secondly, once released into the circulation, it can be used by the liver to produce glucose and glycogen. Thirdly, it has been shown that in the heart muscle lactate acts as an important fuel for the aerobic metabolism. Inactive muscles have also shown an ability to store excess lactate from the circulation.

It might well be that the protons which accompany the production of lactic acid contribute to excessive muscle fatigue in prolonged high intensity endurance exercise.

Of practical importance is that the speed (or exercise intensity) which coincides with the lactate turn point is a reliable guide of the optimum pace which can be maintained for longer periods of time. This is relevant for any endurance event.

Exceeding the speed beyond that of the lactate turn point will result in a rapid depletion of glycogen stores. This will soon result in the need to slow down to accommodate an energy metabolism which has become almost solely dependent on fat and protein as energy sources.

A key reason for Rick Wells' great success is the fact that he possesses a very energy efficient system. (Photo : *New Zealand Triathlete* magazine)

During high intensity exercise which exceeds the lactate turn point, the effects of glycogen depletion can only be temporarily delayed by the consumption of carbohydrate foods and soon excessive muscle fatigue sets in. The athlete experiences this as "hitting the wall".

If the pace, however, is kept just below the intensity by which the lactate turn point occurs, the depletion of glycogen stores takes significantly more time and is further effectively delayed by consumption of high carbohydrate foods during exercise. At the same time there is a significant delay in the onset of exercise muscle fatigue.

Training at intensities close to the lactate turn point results in a delay in the onset of the lactate turn point related to exercise intensity. This is illustrated in Fig. 4.

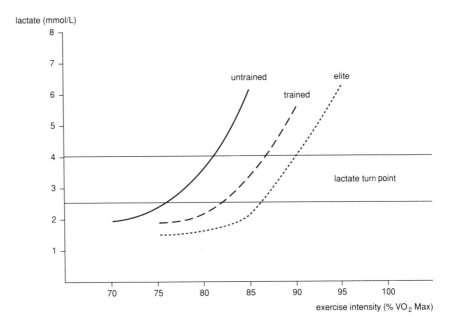

Fig. 4

The lactate turn point is indicated by the fact that there is a rapid accumulation in the muscle, and subsequently the blood stream, of lactic acid. Training will delay the onset of the lactate turn point to a higher exercise intensity.

The lactate turn point is indicated by the fact that there is a rapid accumulation in the muscle cell and subsequently the blood stream of lactic acid. Training will delay the onset of the lactate turn point to a higher exercise intensity.

fuels for endurance exercise

The body has relatively limited supplies of carbohydrate. These are generally distributed in the forms of blood glucose, liver and muscle glycogen. Fat stores contain an abundance of energy which can last us for weeks while protein is only a minor fuel source.

There are four factors that determine which primary fuel, fat or carbohydrate will be utilised for ATP production.

1. exercise intensity

High intensity exercise depends solely on carbohydrate for energy either aerobically or anaerobically.

Aerobic exercise itself can also be looked at as being of higher or lower intensity. When carbohydrates are oxidised, 5.047 calories are derived from one litre of oxygen, while the figure for fat is 4.686. Thus metabolising carbohydrate produces more energy per litre of oxygen which means carbohydrates (glycogen) contribute more to high intensity aerobic energy metabolism than fat. Table 1 illustrates the relationship between exercise intensity and fuel which is being used.

Table 1.

exercise Intensity	fuel used by muscle	examples
low intensity (60-75% VO$_2$ max)	more fat and less carbohydrate	recreational triathlete, Ironman triathlete
moderate intensity (70-85% VO$_2$ max)	more carbohydrate and less fat	competitive triathlete, Half Ironman and Ironman, recreational triathlete (sprint and standard distance)
high intensity (85-100% VO$_2$ max)	mainly carbohydrate	competitive sprint and standard distance triathlete

2. exercise duration

Intensity and duration are inversely related. High intensity exercise can only be sustained for short periods, while low intensity exercise can be maintained for much longer. Fat contributes more energy to low intensity aerobic metabolism. Two sources of fat are available, triglycerides stored in the muscle cell and free fatty acids derived from triglycerides in fat tissue.

3. diet

It has been shown that high carbohydrate diets increase carbohydrate utilisation during exercise. Starvation-type diets, low carbohydrate diets and high fat diets on the other hand, increase the relative contribution of fat to metabolism.

4. training effects

The changes in the muscle cells caused by training will affect the utilisation of the available fuels. The most significant changes appear to occur in response to endurance training. One of the changes is the increased capacity to use fat as a fuel during submaximal levels of exercise. This is due to increased levels of enzymes which break down and oxidise fats.

Table 2. summary of the main characteristics of the human energy systems

	anaerobic alactic	anaerobic lactic	aerobic system (carbohydrate)	aerobic system (fat)
main energy source	phosphagens	muscle glycogen	muscle & liver glycogen	muscle triglycerides and free fatty acids
exercise intensity	very high	high	moderate	low
examples in the triathlon	sprinting, start of triathlon, start of new discipline	hill climb, accelerating	all triathlon events	Half Ironman & Ironman event and any event done at low intensity
rate of ATP production	very high	high	moderate	low
capacity for total ATP production	low	moderate	high	very high
endurance capacity	low	moderate	high	very high
oxygen needs	no	no	yes	yes

At the swim start the anaerobic system comes into play for the competitive triathlete.

4

medical and exercise testing

medical testing

A yearly medical check up for endurance athletes is appropriate. Endurance training puts the body under chronic stress, which can affect the function of the energy systems and the supporting organs. A medical history should include a past and current training history (including goals) to give the medical practitioner an idea of the stresses involved.

The medical examination should have an emphasis on the cardiovascular and musculoskeletal system. The following tests should be included:

1. Height, weight and percentage body fat.

2. Blood pressure, resting pulse rate.

3. Stethoscopic examination of heart and lungs.

4. Peak Flow Rate (a simple measure of lung function).

5. Blood tests are useful including full blood count, sedimentation rate, liver function and kidney function tests, blood sugar, B12, folic acid and iron studies. The last should include ferritin which gives a measure of the iron stores. Additional tests can be ordered as indicated. Trace elements like zinc, copper and magnesium can be measured, but until a normal range has been established for endurance athletes, the results should be treated with caution.

6. Flexibility, especially of the shoulder girdle and lower extremities.

7. Additional tests like X-rays and electrocardiograms need only be done on indication.

exercise testing

The different physical fitness parameters that relate to the triathlon include body composition, strength, speed and endurance. There is a direct relationship between these fitness factors and performance. Flexibility is not a strong performance-related fitness factor although lack of it can contribute to injury and therefore adversely affect performance. Some of the fitness factors can be measured in the laboratory to varying degrees of accuracy.

The triathlete will be mainly interested in the results in relation to their potential in the sport. However, it is not feasible to make accurate predictions of an athlete's potential merely based on exercise test results. Those results in isolation are not specific enough and besides, there are too many factors which contribute to performance, many of which we are as yet unable to measure.

A fitness assessment, however, can be useful for the following reasons:

1. It can identify a triathlete's physical strengths and weaknesses.
2. It can provide baseline data for individual training programme prescriptions.
3. It can give feedback for evaluating the effectiveness of the given programme.
4. It is an educational process by which athletes learn to understand their body and the demands of their sport.

Following is an outline of some of the tests that are appropriate for the triathlete and which are generally available through exercise laboratories, fitness institutes and sports medicine centres.

anthropometry

Anthropometry is defined as measurement of the human body. The relevance of taking anthropometric measurements lies in the fact that body weight and body composition are closely related to athletic performance. Achieving a change in body weight/composition requires careful balancing and monitoring of training and dietary practices. Optimum body composition will contribute significantly to performance. When measuring body composition, the main aim is to measure as accurately as possible the amount of fat tissue we carry versus the amount of non fat tissue (lean body weight). An endurance athlete wants to carry a minimum amount of fat tissue as excess weight. However, a certain amount of body fat is required for health and optimal performance.

Some of the more commonly used methods to assess body composition are height and weight charts, body mass index, skin fold measurements and underwater weighing.

1. height and weight charts
Many charts are available indicating desirable weight ranges for males and females depending on height. Measuring weight is the most commonly used test. However it is also the least accurate. Pure weight does not provide information on body composition. Ideal body weight is not ideal for everyone at a given height, because

of bone and muscle differences. Therefore, weight measurement alone does not differentiate between fat mass and lean body weight.

However, as it is a practical and easily available method, it is appropriate that triathletes use the scales to measure fluctuations in body weight on an ongoing basis as long as the limitations are clear. Baseline weight is best taken after waking up in the morning, before the first workout and breakfast, and preferably following the emptying of the bowel and bladder, wearing little or no clothing. When measuring fluid loss following a hard workout, weight can be measured before and after. The weight difference indicates the amount of fluid lost. Before weighing after exercise, perspiration needs to be dried off the body.

2) body mass index

A commonly used measure of body composition by professionals, especially in overweight people, is the Body Mass Index (BMI). The BMI is derived from body weight and height measurements and the most widely used formula is body weight in kg divided by height, in metres, squared.

$$BMI = \frac{weight \ (kg)}{height^2 \ (m^2)}$$

For example, a man weighing 70 kg who is 1.73 m tall has a BMI of 23.4 kg per square metre. Studies have shown that the BMI correlates well with actual measurement of body fat from underwater weighing. The desirable range of BMI is 20-25 kg per square metre - for young adult men and women.

A BMI of 25-30 indicates overweight, and room for weight reduction.

A BMI in excess of 30 indicates obesity.

The BMI is recommended for adults only.

3) skin fold measurements

Measuring skin fold thickness with the help of callipers is an accurate way of estimating the amount of body fat. Recommended fat percentages for athletes are generally based on actual observations of body fat levels of top athletes in various sports (Table 1).

There is a variety of methods available to estimate body fat percentage through measuring skin folds. Approximately 50 percent of the body storage fat is subcutaneous (under the skin). The measurement of skin folds at various sites of the body, therefore, reflects the amount of this storage fat. A set of skin fold callipers are used to measure the skin folds. Depending on the particular method used, from 2-8 skin folds can be measured. The sum of the skin folds is then used in an equation to estimate the percentage of body fat.

Table 1. **guidelines for acceptable body fat levels**

Essential body fat	Male	3%
	Female	12%
Recommended for competitive endurance sport	Male	5-10%
	Female	12-15%
Recommended for recreational endurance, sport, health & fitness	Male	10-16%
	Female	15-21%

This method is open to abuse if used by people who do not have an understanding of the methods and the importance of accurate measuring. The fact that there is no standardisation in the technique and the interpretation of methods is also a problem. However, it is a useful method if carried out properly as it is quick and inexpensive and done by a trained person, can be relatively accurate. Usually there is a reduction in the measured fat percentage following a period of training. If there is no accompanying weight loss, or if there is an increase in total weight, then this indicates an increase in muscle bulk. This can especially occur in novice triathletes.

4) underwater weighing

Underwater weighing is the most accurate laboratory procedure for measuring body density. This method requires the athlete to be weighed under water as well as on land. Fat is less dense than water and floats. Bone and muscle tissue are higher in density and therefore sink. A person with more fat, therefore, will weigh less under water. By using a standard formula, the volume and density of the body is calculated and then equated to a fat percentage. Underwater weighing is technically a difficult procedure and should only be executed by trained personnel.

maximum oxygen uptake and exercise economy

VO_2 max uptake is defined as the greatest rate at which oxygen can be taken up, distributed and used by the body during physical activity (V = volume of oxygen per minute, O_2 = oxygen and max = represents maximal exercise conditions).

A high level of VO_2 max depends on proper functioning of the respiratory system, cardiovascular system and the musculoskeletal system. VO_2 max is usually expressed in terms of oxygen consumed per minute or by millilitre of oxygen consumed per kilogram body weight per minute (ml/kg/min). By introducing body weight into the equation it becomes possible to compare the VO_2 max of people of varying sizes. One of the limiting factors of VO_2 max is how fast oxygen can be used to produce energy in the working muscle.

VO_2 max is usually tested on a treadmill or bicycle ergometer which allows the progressive increase in workload from light to exhaustive (maximal) exercise. The amount of oxygen consumed during the exercise test is measured using various methods of which the gas flow meter is the most common. The VO_2 max measured is most reliable when the activity closely mimics the activity for which the athlete is trained. Triathletes can, therefore, be tested on either a treadmill or an exercycle.

Most elite male triathletes have a VO_2 max of 60-80 ml/kg/min. Most elite female triathletes have a VO_2 max of 50-70 ml/kg/min.

One of the factors which is responsible for the difference between males and females is that women have a lower oxygen binding capacity of the blood. Additionally, they have a higher body fat content, smaller muscle mass and less powerful muscles.

A high VO_2 max indicates a high level of aerobic fitness resulting in optimal utilisation of aerobic energy systems in the muscle cells. Those aerobic energy systems are by far the most important in endurance events like the triathlon. A high VO_2 max, therefore, indicates potential for endurance exercise.

Our VO_2 max is decided by hereditary factors. Through training, VO_2 max can only be improved by up to fifteen percent. Elite endurance athletes have a higher VO_2 max, but within this group VO_2 max is not a good predictor of race performance. This is where exercise economy (or efficiency) comes in. Exercise economy (efficiency in O_2 utilisation) is the amount of oxygen different athletes require when swimming, biking and running at a given submaximal pace. The exercise efficiency is usually expressed as a percentage of VO_2 max.

Differences in exercise economy in the three disciplines are a contributing factor to differences in race performance in triathletes with a similar VO_2 max. Triathletes with a high VO_2 max, but a poor exercise economy, are less efficient and require more O_2 than average to swim, bike and run at any given speed. Research has shown that exercise economy can be improved through endurance (long distance) training. Most research in this respect has been done on runners and it has been found that running more than 100 km a week will improve running economy.

Exercise economy is especially relevant to the long distance triathlons. Endurance training improves efficiency and, therefore, the ability to go faster without an increase in perceived effort.

Additional factors which will enhance exercise economy, besides endurance training, are improvements in aerodynamics and lightness of equipment. Drafting is also a very effective way of improving economy. In the swim and the run, drafting will improve exercise economy up to 10 percent. In the bike, when drafting close, it can be as high as 30 percent.

lactate turn point (anaerobic threshold) testing

The lactate turn point can be tested in the field or in the laboratory. Following increasing exercise intensities, blood is taken for lactic acid measurements. The heart rate is directly related to exercise intensity. The heart rate by which the lactic acid starts to accumulate is called the lactate turn point (or the anaerobic threshold). This usually coincides with a lactic acid greater than 4 mmol/litre.

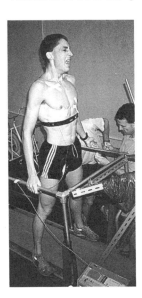

The strain of anaerobic threshold testing.

(See also fig. 4 Chapter 3.)

The problem with anaerobic threshold testing is that the curve is not always that steep. For unknown reasons, some athletes have difficulty raising their lactate levels over 4 mmol/litre despite working extremely hard. Therefore, it is always good to compare the laboratory tests with field tests during training as discussed in chapter 5, "Training Principles". The lactate turn point can be expressed as a percentage of maximum heart rate or a percentage of maximum oxygen uptake.

field testing

VO_2 max has been overvalued in the past as a prediction of endurance performance. For running and cycling a better prediction of potential, measured in the laboratory, is the maximum achieved workload on the treadmill or exercycle rather than the measured VO_2 max.

However, field testing in the way of time trials is still the most specific way of assessing a triathlete's fitness and potential. The distances used are arbitrary as long as it concerns a time trial which takes at least four minutes.
Common time trials used are :

Swimming: 400 metre, 750 metre, 1000 metre or 1500 metre

Cycling: 4 km, 16 km, 25 km, 40 km

Running: 1 mile, 3 km, 5 km or 10 km

If done repeatedly at appropriate times during the training year, time trials are one of the more accurate and controlled ways of measuring progress. The ultimate test, however, is still the race.

5

training principles

Frequency, duration and intensity of training determine the ultimate conditioning of the individual triathlete. Finding the right balance while training for three disciplines is the art and science of the triathlon.

training frequency

Four workouts per week in each discipline (12 workouts in total) will give an improvement of up to 90 percent of your potential (on the condition that these workouts are executed properly). Additional workouts give only a small percentage improvement with the increased risk of injury and overtraining. For this reason it is recommended that the serious triathlete aims for 12 workouts per week. Extra sessions can be undertaken in times of heavy training (for example in the 6-8 weeks before a race) or where extra attention is being given to a weak discipline. Any additional sessions should be "recovery sessions" with an emphasis on low intensity and short duration.

Alternatively, the three rest days per discipline a week can be used for catchup training if part of the programme has been missed for some reason.

A programme based on 12 workouts per week allows for flexibility. Problems with the weather, injury and other commitments can be taken into account without having to sacrifice part of the training programme. A schedule of 15 or 18 workouts is often too tight. This does not allow for flexibility and may cause frustration or anxiety at not being able to achieve your training goals. The superbly fit, high performance athletes will, however, train above the recommended 12 sessions to reach their maximum potential. But, a high level of competitiveness can still be maintained without a significant decline in performance, with up to 12 sessions a week.

Triathletes entering the sport who commence with a low level of fitness will improve their fitness and performance dramatically with two workouts per discipline a week.

They will reach a plateau after approximately 2-3 months. Further improvement will then be achieved only by increasing the frequency of training.

It must be stressed that the less ambitious triathlete can take part comfortably in short distance triathlons (up to 1500 m swim, 40 km cycle and 10 km run) with a routine of two sessions per discipline a week.

training duration

Present theories on exercise suggest that duration of training for the individual discipline should be approximately 100-300 percent of the length or duration of the specific event. In the triathlon this can be slightly less because of the cross-training effect although this principle should not be overestimated.

This means that for a short distance triathlon (1.5 km swim, 40 km cycle and 10 km run) training sessions for the different disciplines will range from a 1.5 km-4 km swim, a 40 km-100 km cycle and a 5 km-25 km run. Some training sessions in the different disciplines will have to be locked together for practical reasons and also to introduce the transition effect.

A competitive triathlete can perform well in a short distance triathlon with approximately 2-3 hours' training a day with slightly longer sessions in the weekend and one rest day during the week. For the recreational triathlete (if there is such a person) who is just aiming to finish, building up to one hour a day, six days a week will be sufficient to finish a short distance event comfortably.

For longer events it becomes practically impossible to spend every day on 100-300 percent of the race time or distance. Here the programme has to be adjusted and built around one long bike ride (4-6 hours) and one long run (2-4 hours) per week. To be competitive in an Ironman event (3.9 km swim, 180 km cycle and 42 km run) you will have to spend 3-6 hours a day training, six days a week.

Research has identified training duration levels that increase the probability of injury as follows: swimming - more than 30 km per week; running - more than 100 km per week; cycling - more than 350 km per week.

These limits have been identified for individual sports but for the triathlon these distances might be slightly less due to the accumulative effect of training in the different disciplines. Obviously you are in the danger zone when training for long distance events.

training intensity

The key to a successful training programme is to know at what pace to train to maximise fitness and racing performance. The principles of duration and frequency of training sessions are relatively clear and will apply to the great majority of triathletes. Opinions on training intensity differ, however, mainly due to the fact that all athletes have their own unique abilities to cope with different levels of training intensity. Here is where individualisation of the training programme comes in and where the athletes have to experiment to find out at what levels they can cope.

Research information on this aspect of training is sparse. Endurance athletes are now starting to train with heart rate monitors as the frequency of the heartbeat can be a reliable indication of the level of training intensity. But, most of us still rely on our experience and intuition when it comes to pacing ourselves through our training. This is a natural way of training which requires continuous awareness of how the body reacts at different levels of exercise intensity.

Pauli Kiuri has training with a heart rate monitor down to a fine art. (Photo: *New Zealand Triathlete* magazine)

We can identify three basic levels of intensity when training for endurance events - low intensity, submaximal or moderate intensity and high intensity training.

1) low intensity training

This is done at a pace which is so easy that you can comfortably maintain a conversation. The heart rate will be between 100-140 beats/minute at which the oxygen uptake will be around 60-75 percent of the VO_2 max, depending on the level of fitness. It is the pace used for warming up and cooling down before and after harder sessions. It is used also for longer, continuous workouts and for shorter recovery sessions. Training at this pace helps recovery and at the same time enhances aerobic capacity. You recover while you train. This does not apply, however, to the weekly or fortnightly long effort. Even though the pace is easy the amount of time spent training is stressful on the body.

Recovery-type training is enjoyable, relatively pain free and is considered low risk as far as injuries are concerned. People who exercise for enjoyment, social reasons or health reasons, should train solely at this pace. For the competitive triathlete also, recovery sessions incorporated in training programmes can be therapeutic.

The principle of low intensity training is especially relevant for running as the nature of the running movement causes a higher risk of injury and overtraining.

This is less relevant for cycling and swimming where the body is cushioned against the effects of gravity.

All training sessions contain an element of low intensity training either as a cool down before or after interval training.

2) submaximal intensity training

This is done at and just below the anaerobic (lactate) threshold, hence its name - Anaerobic Threshold (AT) Training. It is the training intensity when lactic acid starts to accumulate in the working muscle. Once the anaerobic threshold is exceeded, the lactic acid and the accompanying protons in the muscle will interfere with its action and a reduction in performance will follow through an increase in fatigue and muscle soreness. This coincides with the point where the oxygen supply is unable to meet the oxygen demand of the working muscle. Usually this occurs when the oxygen uptake is between 70 and 90 percent of the VO_2 max of the individual.

The level of VO_2 max, as well as the percentage of VO_2 max by which the Anaerobic Threshold is reached, is decided by natural ability - elite runners run at 85-90 percent of their VO_2 max before beginning to accumulate lactic acid - and level of fitness. AT pace is similar to or just below race pace for a 1500 m swim, 40 km bike ride and 10 km run.

Training at, or just below, the anaerobic threshold will increase your VO_2 max as well as shift the anaerobic threshold pace to a higher percentage of VO_2 max. In practical terms this means that you will be able to race at a faster pace without a rapid onset of fatigue and muscle soreness.

The anaerobic threshold concept is rapidly gaining acceptance in endurance sports. AT training is usually done as time trials up to 60 minutes or as interval repetitions lasting four minutes. An easy pace can be maintained in between the repetitions. The elite Ironman triathlete needs to do longer time trials and repetitions than this general recommendation.

The only way to have your AT accurately determined is through testing in a laboratory. By this method the heart rate, which correlates with the AT, indicates the intensity at which you should work out. Laboratory testing is not easily accessible for most triathletes, however, and can be expensive. Unless you have access to an accurate heart rate monitor while training it will still be difficult to judge the ideal pace.

Top athletes seem to have an intuitive tendency to incorporate training sessions at AT pace. They were doing this before the concept of AT training was known. They find, after some trial and error, that by training at a certain submaximal pace they are able to dramatically improve their performance without too much risk of injury and overtraining.

By monitoring your body signals closely you can learn your AT pace. Go for a run on the flat when there is no wind and when you are rested. Slowly increase your speed every minute. There will be a point when suddenly the depth and rate of breathing will increase. It is not possible to have a conversation. There will also be an awareness of the onset of muscle discomfort and fatigue. You are now crossing the anaerobic threshold.

Repeat the exercise while cycling and swimming and start practising intervals at AT pace. Soon you will become familiar with the feeling that you are crossing the anaerobic threshold. AT training is at, or just below, this intensity.

This experiment makes it obvious that training at AT pace requires a lot of control as the pace needs to be even throughout the interval sessions. There is no room for erratic variation in speed as that would diminish the ultimate effect of this concept of training and increase the possibility of injury and overtraining.

A second indicator of the anaerobic threshold is the heart rate. The target heart rate for AT training is between 150 and 190 beats per minute depending on the maximum heart rate, level of fitness, sex and age of the individual. For a trained athlete it is the maximum heart rate minus 10-20 beats. For the untrained athlete it is the maximum heart rate minus 20-40 beats.

To assess your heart rate either use a heart rate monitor or take a pulse count immediately following the effort. This is done best by using the method outlined in Table 1.

Table 1
When you do not have access to a heart rate monitor use the "10 beat time" to assess your heart rate. This is the time in seconds it takes for the heart to beat 10 times. Start timing on the first beat by counting 0,1,2 etc. and stop the time at 10. The heart rate can then be compared with the time in this table.

time	hr	time	hr	time	hr
3.1	194	4.1	146	5.1	118
3.2	188	4.2	143	5.2	115
3.3	182	4.3	140	5.3	113
3.4	177	4.4	136	5.4	111
3.5	171	4.5	133	5.5	109
3.6	167	4.6	130	5.6	107
3.7	162	4.7	128	5.7	105
3.8	158	4.8	125	5.8	103
3.9	154	4.9	122	5.9	102
4.0	150	5.0	120	6.0	100

The maximum heart rate is best established in the laboratory or by exercising (running, cycling or swimming) at maximum effort for approximately five minutes including a sprint for the last 30 seconds. Examples are a one mile run uphill, a 400 metre swim or a five minute hill climb on the bike, all at maximum effort, and sprinting for the last 30 seconds.

This should not be done without supervision unless you have a basic level of fitness and experience and do not suffer from any medical condition.

The maximum heart rate lowers with age. There are great individual differences between maximum heart rates ranging from 160-220 beats per minute. The maximal heart rate is not a reliable indicator for fitness and performance and is not affected by training. Training, however, will lower your resting heart rate and the heart rate at which you exercise, thus improving your efficiency.

3) high intensity training - pace training

This is done at a pace exceeding the anaerobic threshold. Repetitions done at this pace will cause the lactic acid to rise above the anaerobic threshold after 1-2 minutes, depending on the level of fitness. Repetitions of this kind should not exceed three minutes and should have 30 seconds to two minutes recovery time in between. This pace is comparable with a 10 minute time trial done at race pace.

As the repetitions do not exceed three minutes, this means that the pace is still very much controlled. The oxygen uptake will be 90-100 percent of VO_2 max. Research has shown that this type of interval training reveals the greatest increase in VO_2 max. As the anaerobic threshold is exceeded repetitively when we do this type of training it will have a positive effect on the anaerobic threshold. The body will try to delay the onset of lactic acid accumulation by shifting the anaerobic threshold up to the level of VO_2 max.

The importance of training at 90-100 percent of VO_2 max for greatest gains in aerobic power is underestimated.

It needs to be stressed that even for short repetitions, training at an intensity exceeding VO_2 max has no obvious advantage and carries a much higher risk of injury. The recommended heart rate for high intensity training is the maximum heart rate minus 5-20 beats. This type of training should only be attempted by competitive triathletes who have done at least 4-6 weeks of basic conditioning through low intensity and AT training and who are following structured training programmes. The recreational triathlete who is out to last the distance will get by with the more pleasant low intensity training and for variety, some AT training.

The characteristics of three different intensities, their place in training and their effects are summarised in Table 2 on the following page.

summary

The guidelines given in this chapter on duration, frequency and intensity of training are meant to be just that - guidelines. They are based on present research information and the personal experience of the author as a successful triathlete and coach.

Every individual triathlete has their own unique physiological and psychological ability to cope with, and adapt to, different levels of training duration, frequency and intensity. It is the responsibility of individual triathletes, taking these guidelines into consideration, to find the balance which suits their characteristics and particular situation.

For competitive triathletes in general, the recommended frequency of training is

Table 2.	low intensity training	submaximal (moderate) intensity training	high intensity training
% of VO$_2$ max	60-75%	70-90%	85-100%
% of race pace for a 1.5-km; 40-km; 10-km event	<70%	70-90%	90-110%
heart rate beats per min	Maximum heart rate minus 40-80 beats	Maximum heart rate minus 20-40 beats	Maximum heart rate minus 5-20 beats
lactate level in the blood	Low	Low	High
subjective pace	Easy - conversation pace	Medium to hard - difficult to converse	Hard to very hard - unable to converse
training effect	· Assists recovery · Basic aerobic conditioning · Familiarisation of body systems with endurance exercise · Warming up/cooling down	Increases anaerobic threshold Increases VO$_2$ max	Increases VO$_2$ max Increases anaerobic threshold
type of training	Continuous	Long intervals - 4 mins or more Time trials (20-60 mins)	Short intervals - 3 mins or less
approx. duration of training per session	20 mins-5hrs	10-60 mins of interval or time trial training, preceded by warm up and followed by cool down	10-30 mins of interval training preceded by warm up and followed by cool down
frequency of training sessions per week*	Swim 1 Cycle 2-3 Run 2-4	Swim 2-4 Cycle 2-3 Run 1-2	Swim 1-3 Cycle 0-1 Run 0-1

*All training sessions have an element of low intensity training, either continuous or as a warm up or cool down.

four sessions per discipline a week. The recreational triathlete will get by with two sessions per discipline per week. The duration of these sessions is between 100 and 300 percent of the length or duration of the event for which you are training. This applies especially for the short distance triathlon (up to 1500 metre swim, 40 km cycle, 10 km run). Training at the right intensity is of the utmost importance in order to achieve maximum performance.

6

training methods

In this chapter the practical implications of the theoretical outline on training principles are discussed. Duration, frequency and intensity of training are affected by different training methods. Although the range of training methods used for the three disciplines is the same, the emphasis will differ.

endurance training (distance training)

Distance training is done solely to enhance endurance - the ability to withstand prolonged strain. It is done at a continuous pace of low intensity (conversation pace) and for a duration close to or exceeding the length of the specific event you are training for. The longer the event the more important this training session becomes. For example, when training for an Ironman event the rest of the training programme will be built around the long bike ride and the long run. Distance training will familiarise the body with the effects of endurance exercise.

This physical and mental conditioning of the body before an event will dramatically reduce the risk of "hitting the wall". The body will not enter into strange territory and will be able to anticipate the special metabolic demands which become so crucial towards the latter parts of the bike and run sections.

Each discipline will usually have one distance session per week. When training for short distance triathlons the swim will be 30-60 minutes, the bike ride up to three hours and the run approximately 90 minutes. When training for an Ironman event the swim will be 60-90 minutes, the bike ride up to six hours and the run up to four hours. Distance training for swimming is optional for the short distance but recommended for the long distance events.

It must be remembered that attaining these distances is done through a gentle build up towards the desired time, depending on the level of fitness and experience of the athlete at the onset of the programme.

recovery training

This is done mainly to help the body recover from harder workouts. It is done at a continuous, low intensity pace, but for a shorter period of time than the distance training and consequently avoids prolonged strain.

Recovery training is especially relevant in running where the pounding exposes us to muscle soreness and injury. It is least practised in swimming. Swimmers are well known for their gruelling workouts of long duration and relatively high intensity day after day. The buoyancy of the water and the smoothness of the swimming movement protects them from stress injury.

When we run four times a week we will have at least two recovery runs. When running five or six times a week we will have three recovery runs and two or three harder sessions. This is based on the hard day/easy day principle so well known in running circles.

It appears to take the body more than 24 hours to recover completely from a hard workout even when we are fully fit. Training hard every day will have an accumulative effect to the point of injury and breakdown. This applies to a lesser degree to cycling and swimming.

Recovery training can be done either by itself or following a hard workout. An easy 20-30 minute swim or bike ride following a hard run can be soothing for aching muscles and it enhances the removal of waste products from the muscles.

For practical reasons it is best to apply the "hard day/easy day" principle not only in the run but also for the bike ride. As we use different muscle groups in these two sports we can alternate a hard running day and a hard cycling day with an easy bike ride and run as optional recovery sessions. Recovery training can also be done to maintain basic fitness. This is further outlined in the chapter on training programmes.

steady state training

This is a continuous type of training at a pace higher than the recovery pace, but below the AT pace. Some triathletes prefer to do their distance training and some of their recovery sessions at this pace to try and mimic the race conditions more closely.

In general, triathletes with a running background are able to do their easier running sessions and distance training at a steady state pace without coming to grief. Cyclists can do the same for similar cycling sessions. Years of training have increased their body resistance and they have overcome the need for easy recovery sessions. Distance training, however, especially for the long distance event done at a steady pace, requires close monitoring of the body signals and adjustments of the pace accordingly.

For the triathlete, the pace of recovery sessions and distance training will depend on your background in the relevant discipline, your current level of fitness and your personal preference.

speed training

This is done as interval training or in the form of time trials at, below or just above AT level. Longer intervals (four minutes or more) are done at submaximal intensity. Shorter intervals (three minutes or less) are done at higher intensity or submaximal intensity depending on the level of fitness. Time trials are usually done for 10-60 minutes at submaximal pace. Serious Ironman triathletes can exceed this time.

Remember that you must never train at maximum (sprint) speed. Always be in control of your pace.

By using shorter rest periods (15-60 seconds) between the intervals, speed and endurance will be enhanced. As fitness increases, rest periods should be shortened to obtain this dual benefit of speed training.

If we swim four times a week, at least three sessions will have an element of speed training. Repetitions range from 25-800 metres depending on the ability, level of fitness and how you feel on the day.

Common examples of AT training are: 2-4 x 400 m (one minute rest); 3-6 x 300 m (one minute rest); 200 m, 400 m, 600 m (800 m), 600 m, 400 m, 200 m with one minute rest in between - this is called a sausage hierarchy in which you increase then decrease the duration of your repetitions; time trials can vary between 400 and 3000 m. Repetitions below 200 m are usually done at the higher intensity speeds.

If we cycle four times a week, at least two sessions will have an element of speedwork. For example, 4-8 x two minutes acceleration at submaximal or high intensity or ascending 4-6-8 and descending 8-6-4 minutes at AT pace - again the sausage hierarchy all with one minute easy cycling in between.

A cycling time trial at AT pace up to 60 minutes is not only a good combination of speed and endurance training, it is also a good way of monitoring improvement. This should be done at the most, once a week.

Some cyclists train occasionally at very high speeds (45-50 km/hr) behind motorcycles to improve their basic speed. This type of pace training requires a high level of concentration and skill and should only be attempted by the more experienced cyclist/triathlete.

If we run four times a week usually one session will be spent on interval training. Repetitive accelerations anywhere between two and eight minutes can be done with one minute of easy jogging in between. Ascending/descending interval sessions (2-4-6-(8)-6-4-2 minutes) at AT pace over varied terrain (golf courses, parks, forest walks) give the training session variety. Repetitions can be done on the track between 800 m and 3200 m (1/2-2 miles). Mile repetitions (3-5 times at AT pace) have become the standard way of monitoring fitness and progress for many triathletes. Before doing speed training make sure you have a sound basic fitness and remember to build up the intervals gradually.

In general, the longer the event you train for, the more time you will spend on the submaximal type of speed training, rather than high intensity training. Be prepared to experiment with the different speed levels so that you can monitor how you are coping mentally as well as physically. Check how much recovery you require in between intervals and try to shorten this progressively. The main aim is to maintain an even pace through the sessions. If fatigue sets in too soon the pace will falter. This can be corrected by shortening the intervals and/or prolonging the rest periods and/or lowering your speed.

Speed training is an important tool in trying to achieve maximum performance in racing but it will also expose you to risk of injury and overtraining if it is not done properly. Be flexible and be prepared to lower the intensity of your training if this is what your body tells you.

strength training - resistance training

Hardly a sport exists where athletes do not benefit from increased strength and the triathlon is no exception. Strength training not only adds strength but it also improves the muscular endurance and helps prevent injury. Strength training is most effective if it is specific, which means that it should mimic the movement pattern of the sport we train for as closely as possible. It is difficult to achieve this using weights and machines, which makes weight training of limited value for the triathlete.

As weight training is not specific enough it should never replace a run, bike or swim session. Here the time factor comes in. Most triathletes are struggling to complete their 12 recommended training sessions, as the triathlon is one of the most time consuming sports.

In the off season weight training can be done to maintain general fitness (do frequent repetitions with light weights) or to strengthen specific muscle groups.

Contrary to weight training, strength training can be easily incorporated into the normal training sessions. Strength training is usually done at submaximal or high intensity pace and has the added advantage of improving endurance. It is achieved by increasing resistance when we are swimming, cycling or running. This can be done by swimming with the arms only. The body drag can be increased by wearing a rubber band around the ankles causing the legs to drop and the use of pull buoys - a pair of foam cylinders tied together with a rope held between the thighs. Hand paddles can be used to strengthen shoulder muscles because they increase the pulling surface area. They have to be used with care, however, as they can cause the dreaded "swimmer's shoulder".

Cycling into a head wind and up a hill is a form of strength training especially when bigger gears are used. Alternatively, an ergometer (stationary bicycle) with wind or magnetic resistance can be used - an excellent and specific way of strength training.

If you spend 30-60 minutes on an ergometer you can simulate a hard workout especially when interval type training is done using increasingly higher gears (**see Chapter 11, "Cycling"**).

Hill repetitions (a common training modality in running) are rarely done by cyclists. This is probably because hill repetitions require a tremendous amount of discipline and psychological strength. Most triathletes would agree that it is harder to cycle up a hill than to run, especially when we try to do it hard. To reach the top with aching thighs and with the knowledge that you have to go back down to do it again can be soul destroying. Perhaps that is why it is such an effective training method. It not only increases muscular strength but also mental discipline and toughness.

The pace should be controlled, usually anywhere between submaximal pace (for the longer hills taking 6-20 mins) and high intensity pace (for the shorter steeper hills). Work loads can be adjusted with gear changes. The secret is to maintain the same effort throughout the interval session with the easy downhill in between to recover.

Strength training in running can also be done by hill repetitions on the same principle, but by using slightly shorter intervals. High intensity sessions up to two minutes or moderate intensity up to 10 minutes can be used. Again, trial and error will teach you which pace is right and over a period, times will gradually come down as strength improves.

Another type of strength training is running in sandhills. Battling up and down the loose sand for 20-30 minutes at submaximal to high intensity pace will give you an excellent workout. The loose sand prevents jarring, and injury is unlikely despite the high workload. This will also strengthen the ankles which is an added benefit for those who have a tendency to sprain easily.

Plyometrics is a type of strength training which improves explosive strength. Plyometrics involves hopping, jumping and bounding exercises which are extremely good for improving muscle contractility. Plyometric exercises are running specific with some carry over to cycling. Many triathletes tend to lose the spring in their running during times of heavy training or frequent competition. This might well be caused by running frequently in a fatigued state thus lowering muscle contractility of the muscle groups involved. Including some plyometrics in running training can assist in keeping the spring in your stride.

Strength training done in the way described is a hard but effective method of increasing fitness and performance in a short period of time. Undertaking such a quality schedule often means that the total mileage in training can be reduced without affecting the standard of fitness.

Strength training improves not only strength, endurance and speed but above all physical and mental toughness, essential qualities for the more serious athletes.

technique training

The techniques in the three disciplines of the triathlon will be discussed in their respective chapters. Running and cycling we learn as children and as they involve a relatively simple pattern of movement, usually only minor adjustments are needed to improve efficiency.

Swimming, however, is different. As children we are taught how to swim, but mainly for survival. As the pattern of movement is complicated, proper coaching in technique is required to improve style and efficiency. This can only be done with the help of a qualified coach. This is why triathletes with a background in swimming and who were swimming competitively at a young age have such an advantage over their rivals who still have to acquire the basic swimming skills. But with time, practice and determination we have seen many runners and cyclists become competent swimmers able to restrict the time they lose in the swim to a minimum.

Training sessions on technique are never wasted. Obviously, this should be done mainly in the off-season and pre-season. When training hard we have to remind ourselves continually about style and technique as a loss in style will immediately result in a loss of form. If this happens, technique training immediately becomes a high priority even if it occurs in the weeks leading up to a race. Faults easily grow into habits and correcting them becomes even harder.

transition training

To familiarise ourselves with that awkward feeling when we change from one pattern of movement to another, we have to practise this aspect of the triathlon. To do this, at least one training session every week in the period before an event should consist of a swim, cycle and run in an unbroken sequence. To save time, many triathletes do "back to back" sessions - run or bike to the pool, have a swim then bike or run back home as part of their training.

To gain the maximum training effect, hard sessions should preferably be done when an athlete is rested. This can then be followed by a recovery session in a different discipline, for example a hard bike ride followed by an easy 20-30 min. run. As you generally will have only one or two hard running sessions, a run before or after a swim will be satisfactory.

There is still little scientific information available on the importance of transition training, how often we should practise it and in what way. As there are no hard and fast rules, much will depend on personal preference and hence allowances can be made for lifestyle and other commitments.

fatigue training

This type of training should be done only by the more experienced and seasoned triathlete as fatigue training involves an increase in training intensity or duration at a stage in the training session where the body is already feeling fatigued. It applies to the long distance triathletes in particular.

Fatigue training will condition the body to burn fat which is available in limitless supply, rather than glycogen. It also familiarises the body and mind with fatigue - you can train yourself to tolerate fatigue.

Distance training is a form of fatigue training, especially when done at a steady state pace rather than the easier "recovery pace". Larger or prolonged interval sessions usually require a little more effort towards the end and automatically introduce fatigue training. A hard bike ride can be followed by a longer run but this should not be done too often (at the most once every two or three weeks). Hill repetitions, where cycling and running up hill are alternated, involve a combination of strength training, transition training and fatigue training.

Fatigue sessions should be mainly incorporated into a training programme in the 6-8 weeks leading up to an event. However, they should not be done within 10 days of an event.

Hill training is very effective at improving strength, speed and endurance.

7

planning and periodisation

planning a training year

Planning a training year depends on the following factors:

1. Level of competence. This relates to the triathlete's strengths and weaknesses. Non-swimmers, for example, will initially have to spend more time on that discipline all year round until satisfactory improvements have been made.

2. Training age. Training age needs to be distinguished from chronological age. A 19-year-old triathlete who has trained consistently for four years has a different (harder) programme from a 24-year-old novice.

3. Goal setting. Goal setting is crucial when planning a training and competition year. The difference in programmes for highly competitive triathletes and triathletes who take part for health, fitness and fun only, is enormous.

4. Important competitions. The distinction needs to be made between key races (e.g. national championships, selection races, "money" races) and lead-up races as mental and physical preparation will be different.

5. Individual requirements of the athlete. This refers to individualising training programmes to suit the individual triathlete. This is mostly the responsibility of the individual athlete.

6. The ability to reach and maintain top form. This will decide if an athlete will aim at a series of races or one or two key events only.

When structuring a training year, there are some universally accepted principles which need to be clearly understood by the athlete and coach.

- Initially, improvement only occurs if training is progressively increased.

However, the increase in training must follow a pattern of load and recovery, in which stresses must be followed by periods of restoration.

If there is no allowance made for sufficient recovery, continued training stress can lead to a drop in performance (the first sign of overtraining/or injury).

The body adapts best to a training load with variations in the degree of loading and changes in the type of loading and intensity. This is where periodisation comes in.

periodisation

Training specificity is the most important training principle. Specificity is related first of all to movement patterns and secondly to the intensity and duration of the specific movement patterns. Intensity, duration and also frequency of training can be varied and movement patterns can be broken down, e.g. by doing drills, specific strength work and technique training.

The athlete can do two things when establishing "when to do what".

1. Set down clear short term and long term goals.

2. Break the year into periods, during which different aspects of the required performance components are being trained. This is called periodisation.

Three distinct periods can be recognised when segmenting the year, the preparation period, the competition period and the transition period. Each period has a different objective and is divided into subphases. An example of a periodisation plan for a triathlete is given in Table 1. The major differences between the periods and subphases are the volume and intensity of training. This is illustrated in Fig. 1.

Table 1.

Northern Hemisphere	Southern Hemisphere		
January	August		
February	September	General Preparation Phase	
March	October		Preparation Period
April	November	Specific Preparation Phase	
May	December	Early Season Competition Phase	
June	January		Competition Period
July	February	Main Season Competition Phase	
August	March		
September	April	Recovery Phase	
October	May		Transition Period
November	June	Specific Development Phase	
December	July	(Single Discipline Phase)	

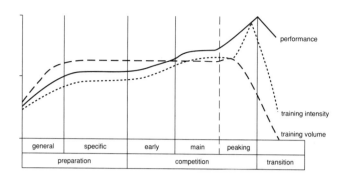

Fig. 1.

A plan for a simple periodisation year (variations in macro and micro cycles have not been indicated).

On a more detailed scale the different phases can be divided into macro cycles (usually between four and eight weeks), which in turn are divided into micro cycles (usually one week). This cyclic type of training pattern makes it possible to introduce shorter or longer periods of training that allows us to make changes in training volumes, training intensities and recoveries.

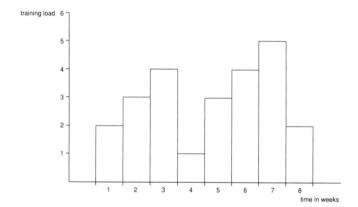

Fig. 2.

An example of a 4-week cyclic training programme.

The principle of cyclic training is outlined in Fig. 2 where a four-week macro cycle is divided into weekly micro cycles. The fourth micro cycle represents recovery. Many variations on this model exist, depending on the stage within the periodisation and individual needs of the athlete. **(See also Chapter 8, "Training Programmes".)**

The objectives of the different training phases mentioned during the year are as follows:

1. general preparation phase
The aim of this phase is to establish a solid foundation for the work that will follow. The general preparation phase can stretch up to four months. It should not be hurried, but gradually build to the training and competition ahead. The volume must be relatively high and should be increased step by step. Intensity varies between low and medium and the emphasis is on developing general physical performance capacities (especially endurance and strength). This is also a time to concentrate on technique and correcting major faults.

2. specific preparation phase

The emphasis is on developing sports specific performance capacities. The specific preparation phase is usually about two months. It is a very difficult phase as basic conditioning and more specific training must be balanced according to individual needs. The volume is slightly increased until the middle stages of this phase after which it is maintained or slightly reduced. Intensity is progressively increased. The emphasis is gradually changed from the development of general performance capacities to development of sports specific fitness. Attention needs to be paid to maintaining technique while increasing intensity.

3. early season competition phase

The main objective of this phase is to reach close to top form through a progressively increased competition intensity and gradually improved performances. Sports specific training continues with a high intensity, but a reduced volume. This phase usually lasts two months. Care must be taken that the athlete will not be exhausted by too many competitions, particularly in the latter part of this phase. The training volume is reduced but the intensity remains relatively high. Sports specific physical conditioning reaches the maintenance stage. Techniques should be maintained while specific preparations take place before competition which, at this stage, is seen as part of training. Some tapering can be used in the latter stages of this phase, depending on the importance of the race.

4. main season competition phase

The aim is to produce the optimal performance of the year allowing for a short recovery from the early season competition phase followed by specific preparation for the targeted event (peaking). The main competition phase should not be shorter than six weeks in order to allow for recovery and preparation for the peak. The key factor here is to find the right number of competitions prior to the climax event. The recovery, combined with a short cycle of specific conditioning, should re-establish basic performance capacities.

In this early stage of the main competition phase the training is of low intensity and medium volume. This is then followed by a low volume, high intensity period in the second part of the phase. Maintenance of technique again is crucial. It is too late, however, to make major changes to technique. The number of lead-up competitions to the climax event must be kept to a minimum to avoid psychological fatigue.

There should be at least a week between the last lead-up competition and the climax event. In the main competition phase we can follow the plan of transition, general preparation, specific preparation and competitive phases, scaled down to be fitted into a short period (Fig. 3). The following is a six week example:

week 1 (transition phase)

Recovery and low intensity, medium volume training.

week 2/3 (general preparation phase)
Low intensity, with high volume training, changing to a high intensity and reduced volume as the phase progresses.

week 4/5 (specific preparation phase)
High intensity training, possibly including preliminary competition approximately 7-10 days prior to the major event.

week 6 (competition phase)
This is the pre-competition week which consists of competition specific training (tapering and rest).

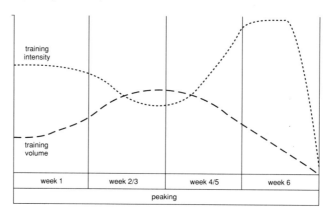

Fig. 3.

The concept of peaking.

Alternatively, the main competitive phase can be planned on a purely cyclic regime planned around key races.

peaking
The general recommendation for tapering for any major event is to reduce training volume a week to 10 days before the event. Most athletes also reduce training intensity. However, there is some evidence that maintaining high intensity training until the day of the main event will assist and improve performance. If this is done, then it is essential that the total volume of training is significantly lowered at the same time. The mechanism behind the relationship between high intensity training up to the day of the event and performance is not quite clear.

The concept of peaking is illustrated in week 5 and 6 of Fig. 3.

5. recovery phase
The transition phase is usually one to two months and aims for psychological and physiological recovery. It should also include an assessment of the year completed and planning of the next training year. The recovery should be active to prevent a drastic drop in physical performance capacities. All sessions should be easy while the frequency of the sessions will drop significantly to 2-3 per week. This is also a time when the athlete can engage in other unrelated, but low risk, physical activities.

6. specific development phase (single discipline phase)

During this phase, training should focus on specific aspects of the triathlon. For the younger and novice athlete this means working on a weak discipline.

Three or four months training (and racing) in only one of the three disciplines can result in significant improvements. The other disciplines can be ignored at this time or they can be maintained by one or two sessions per week. For the more experienced triathlete it might mean working on a specific performance related factor, e.g. strength or technique.

For the elite athlete who has competed for some time, including overseas during the off season, this can also be a good time to have a complete break. Alternatively, it can become part of the general preparation phase. For the social triathlete the off season can happily be spent on the most enjoyable discipline.

double periodisation

Currently, distinction can be made between single and double periodisation. Single periodisation aims at one performance peak in the whole training year, preceded by a competition period. Double periodisation aims at two performance peaks during the training year, both preceded by competition periods. A good example is the triathlete who competes in the Northern Hemisphere as well as the Southern Hemisphere season or the athlete who wants to combine triathlons in the summer and duathlons in the winter. In this model the specific development phase is not included and following the recovery phase the athlete will go straight into the general preparation phase.

Double periodisation should only be used by experienced athletes as it involves more frequent and, therefore, greater training stresses. Double periodisation avoids a long period of non-competition, which in some athletes can cause loss of motivation, commitment and perseverance. In younger athletes, double periodisation can interfere with the long term harmonious development of the athlete and can also contribute to the burn-out syndrome. Too frequent competition in the first competition period will lead to an automatic lowering of the desired training volume in the first phase of the second periodisation period. This can have a negative effect on expected peak performance in the second competition period.

8

training programmes

Before establishing a training programme, determine your goals and your level of motivation. Do you enter the sport to lose weight (there are easier ways) or do you want to compete at a high level?

Many people enter the sport because of the challenge to finish a triathlon and when they find they like the sport they go on to compete more seriously, or to make tri-fitness a part of their lifestyle, adjusting their goals as they go along. The triathlon requires more time and dedication than most sports, even at a recreational level. For the shorter events, a certain amount of basic conditioning is required as opposed to a social game of tennis.

The most balanced triathletes are those who have made training and fitness part of their lifestyle. They are in the minority, however. Most triathletes are denied this luxury as they are limited by family commitments and a full-time job, so if your goals exceed your capabilities, you will become frustrated easily. Although no official figures have been published, there are indications that the dropout rate is high and the growth capability limited in this sport, because such a considerable level of commitment is required. But, with realistic goalsetting and careful planning of a training programme, the triathlon can be an immensely enjoyable and satisfying sport.

The training programmes mentioned in this chapter are examples used successfully by individual triathletes. To cater for the different levels of participation, a wide range of programme examples is offered. Once you have found the programme that resembles your goals and level of motivation, study it in detail and use it as a base to build your own programme. Never make the mistake of copying the programme of a successful triathlete expecting it to work for you as well. Every triathlete has their own unique constitution and level of training which requires adjustments to existing programmes.

The basic principles and methods of training, as outlined in the previous chapters, are what the programmes have in common. It is well known that it will take 4-6 years of serious training before a maximum performance level is achieved, so do not expect immediate results.

In setting yourself a training programme, be aware of your body's strengths and weaknesses. The speed of progress will differ for each discipline depending on natural ability and training input.

preparation period (pre-season training)

A solid build up is required before specific training can begin. The time this takes depends on the background of the athlete. It can take from 4-6 weeks for the elite athlete coming from a winter layoff, to 3-4 months for the novice triathlete. The emphasis will be on aerobic fitness which means that all the sessions are done at a strictly contrQlled and restrained level and at an aerobic (easy) pace. Initial sessions should not last longer than 20-40 minutes. As you build your aerobic base your cardiovascular system will improve its ability to supply your muscles with oxygen. As the oxygen delivery system improves, you can increase, gradually, the duration of your training. As well as increasing aerobic power, this type of training will strengthen the musculoskeletal system without the risk of injury and the chances of a physical breakdown in the form of injury are reduced when more intense training is done at a later stage.

Aerobic training is probably the most enjoyable and rewarding form of training. It is done at a continuous aerobic pace and does not hurt except perhaps for light muscle soreness in the first few weeks. Many people who exercise for enjoyment will never get past this stage of training and because of the limited amount of stress involved are able to do it the year round. This is perfectly acceptable and perhaps a more sensible approach to exercise.

In general, 2-4 sessions a week per discipline should be done at low intensity with a slow increase in duration. The duration can be increased more quickly for swimming and cycling than for running.

An example of a pre-season aerobic build up programme, starting with Week 1 through to Week 8, is given below.

pre-season aerobic build up programme for a more competitive triathlete

week 1	swim	cycle	run
monday	20 mins		20 mins
tuesday		45 mins	
wednesday		60 mins	
thursday	20 mins		20 mins
friday		rest day	
saturday	20 mins	45 mins	
sunday			30 mins

Training is gradually increased in weeks 2-8.

week 8	swim	cycle	run
monday	45-60 mins	1 hr	1 hr
tuesday	45-60 mins	2 hrs	
wednesday			1 hr
thursday	45-60 mins	1 hr 30 mins	
friday		rest day	
saturday	30-45 mins	1 hr	30-35 mins
sunday			75 mins

Comments

* The duration of training is built up gradually over the weeks.
* The intensity of the training is always below submaximal; e.g. heart rate not exceeding the lactate threshold.
* The bike and run sessions especially are of a continuous, aerobic nature.
* The swimming sessions are usually varied, especially when you swim in a squad with a mixture of training methods. At this stage, avoid speed training and do repetitions below submaximal intensity. Much emphasis can be given to swimming technique.
* This programme should be adapted to each individual. Days can be swapped but try to divide the different disciplines over the week. If, for example, you have done more cycling in the off-season, carry on with longer and harder cycling sessions while introducing an aerobic programme as shown here for running and swimming, etc.
* The time required for aerobic work to arrive at a basic level of fitness differs from a few weeks for the experienced triathlete to many months for the overweight novice triathlete.

competition period (in-season training)

This period starts approximately 6-8 weeks before your first event and finishes the day of your last event. The programmes offered in this section cater for a wide range of triathletes with different aspirations and abilities. If you are a recreational triathlete, remember that you will be able to finish a short triathlon comfortably with an aerobic programme of 2/3 sessions per discipline per week as long as you do not race faster than you train. If you are more competitive and look for improvement you will be required to do more specific training, using the different training methods as outlined in Chapter 6.

From a base of aerobic training approximately 6-8 weeks of more specific training is required to prepare for competition in a short distance event (1.5 km, 40 km, 10 km).

For long distant events 8-10 weeks of more specific training, especially in regard to distance training, is required, not only to compete but also to finish an event easily.

Specific training for short distance triathlons can be maintained during the season with short periods of tapering before events, and rest following them. Training for long distance events (up to five hours per day) should only be done for two months at a time. No more than two of these long distance events a year should be done as the risk of fatigue, injury and boredom are relatively high.

The following programmes are examples only and should be adapted to individual training needs so long as the "hard day/easy day" principle for the bike and run is maintained. A considerable amount of hill work is included as hill training is an effective way of improving strength, endurance and toughness. If there are no hills available you are at a disadvantage but by using a headwind and low gears in cycling, or kneelifts, soft sand or staircases in running, you will still be able to build up strength. Be inventive and if necessary go beyond the classic methods of training.

Have one rest day a week that you can use as such or to catch up on 1 or 2 sessions you may have missed earlier in the week. The principle of a rest day makes your programme so much more flexible and at the same time allows for much-needed recovery, especially if it involves specific training for competition. The real addict who cannot cope with a rest day can indulge in 1 or 2 sessions at an easy pace to help get them through the day.

In some of the following programmes a preferential order of training has been indicated, but it is not essential that you hold to this. The bracketed sessions are optional, and always at an easy pace.

Examples of in-season triathlon training programmes:

1. recreational or beginner triathlete - short distance (1.5 km, 40 km, 10 km) triathlon

	swim	cycle	run
monday	(45 mins)		
tuesday		60-90 mins	
wednesday			45 mins
thursday	45 mins	(60 mins)	
friday		rest day	
saturday	30 mins	30 mins	30 mins
sunday			(60 mins)
approx. time	2 hrs	2 hrs 30 mins-3 hrs	2 hrs 15 mins
approx. distance	2-3 km	50-80 km	20-30 km

Comments

* Two sessions per discipline a week is the minimum amount of training required for somebody who possesses the basic skills for the three sports, though three sessions is preferable. This needs to be done for at least six weeks before an event.

* The training is done solely at an aerobic (easy) pace.
* The actual event should be done at a similar pace.
* Any extra time available should be spent on the weakest discipline or the discipline you enjoy most.
* Do at least two continuous open water swims of 30-40 minutes before the event.
* Do the Saturday session in continuous fashion. This is to get used to the transition effect.

2. competitive triathlete - short distance (1.5 km, 40 km, 10 km) triathlon

	swim	cycle	run
monday	1 hr-1 hr 30 mins (1)	(1 hr)(3)	1 hr-1 hr 30 mins intervals (2)
tuesday	1 hr-1 hr 30 mins (1)	2-4 hrs steady state (2)	(15-30 mins) (3)
wednesday	(1 hr) (3)	1 hr 30 mins-2 hrs hills (2)	1 hr 30 mins hill reps (1)
thursday	1 hr-1 hr 30 mins (1)	2 hrs including 40-50 mins time trial (2)	
friday		rest day	
saturday	30-45 mins open water (1)	90-120 mins (2)	30-60 mins (3)
sunday			75-90 mins hill run
approx. time	3 hrs 30 mins-5 hrs 30 mins	7 hrs-10 hrs 30 mins	4-6 hrs
approx. distance	12-20 km	160-300 km	60-80 km

Comments

* If executed properly, this is a strenuous programme. Allow for plenty of recovery and try to have one rest day.
* Swimming, preferably, should be done with a squad.
* The long bike ride on Tuesday is done between an easy and submaximal (steady state) pace.
* The long run on Sunday is done at an easy pace.
* Some triathletes prefer to do the long bike ride on the Sunday as it takes more time than the long run.
* The elite triathlete can include the optional sessions and train for the longer duration.
* Do the Saturday session in continuous fashion to get used to the transition effect.

3. recreational triathlete - long distance (3.8 km, 180 km, 42 km) triathlon

	swim	cycle	run
monday	(1 hr)		1 hr 30 mins
tuesday	1 hr	(2-3 hrs hills)	
wednesday			3 hrs easy
thursday	1 hr	1-2 hrs	(1 hr)
friday		rest day	
saturday	30-60 mins open water	2-3 hrs	1 hr 30 mins
sunday		4-6 hrs	
approx. time	3 1/2-4 hrs	11-15 hrs	7 hrs
approx. distance	10-14 km	220-450 km	60-100 km

Comments

* Except for the swimming where longer intervals can be done, most sessions will be done at a continuous easy pace.
* The emphasis of the training will be on duration rather than intensity as the main aim is to finish the event.
* Any extra time available can be spent on your weak discipline or the discipline you enjoy most.
* Eat and drink during the Saturday morning session and the longer bike sessions. Drink during the running sessions of greater than one hour. Belts are available in which you can carry bottles.
* Experiment with different types of food and fluid to suit your individual requirements **(see also chapter 15, "Nutrition")**. This is an important part of your training, as it will enhance recovery and prevent problems like hypoglycaemia (low blood sugar), dehydration, exhaustion and excessive fatigue.
* Do the Saturday session in continuous fashion.

4. competitive triathlete - long distance (3.8 km, 180 km, 42 km) triathlon

	swim	cycle	run
monday	1 hr 30 mins (1)	1-2 hrs easy (3)	1 hr 30 mins with intervals (2)
tuesday	1 hr 30 mins (1)	2-3 hrs hills (2)	1 hr easy (3)
wednesday	(30 mins easy) (3)	(1 hr easy) (2)	2-4 hours hills (1)
thursday	1 hr 30 mins (1)	3-4 hrs with intervals or hill reps (2)	45 mins (3)
friday	(1 hr)	rest day	
saturday	45-60 mins open water (1)	2-3 hrs (2)	1 hr 30 mins (3)
sunday		4-6 hrs	(30-45 mins)
approx. time	5-7 hrs	12-19 hrs	6-10 hrs
approx. distance	15-20 km	400-600 km	80-140 km

Comments

* This programme is built around a 3-hour run and a 4-6 hour bike ride. As there is so much time involved there will be little left for other commitments and any spare time, preferably, should be spent recovering (eating, drinking, resting).
* Allowance for recovery will determine the success of such a heavy programme.
* This type of programme should be followed by a well-conditioned triathlete only, who has extensive basic experience and conditioning in the three disciplines.
* Eating and drinking during the longer cycling session and the session on Saturday morning, as well as on the longer runs, is of the utmost importance to enhance recovery and prevent problems of exhaustion, dehydration, etc.
* Experiment at these sessions with different foods and fluids to find out about your individual needs.
* Do the Saturday session in continuous fashion.

5. recreational triathlete - middle distance (2 km, 80 km, 21 km) triathlon

	swim	cycle	run
monday	(45 mins-1 hr)		1 hr
tuesday		2-3 hrs	
wednesday			1 hr 30 mins-2 hrs
thursday	45 mins-1 hr		(45 mins-1 hr)
friday		rest day	
saturday	45 mins-1 hr open water	2 hrs	1 hr-1 hr 30 mins
sunday		3-4 hrs	
approx. time	3-4 hrs	7 hrs 30 mins-9 hrs	4 hrs 15 mins-5 hrs 30 mins
approx. distance	6-14 km	160-330 km	40-70 km

Comments   (See 3, recreational triathlete - long distance)

6. competitive triathlete - middle distance (2 km, 80 km, 21 km) triathlon

	swim	cycle	run
monday	1 hr-1 hr 30 mins (1)	1-2 hrs easy (3)	1 hr 30 mins intervals (2)
tuesday	1 hr-1 hr 30 mins (1)	2-3 hrs hills (2)	1 hr easy (3)
wednesday	(30 mins easy) (3)	1 hr easy (2)	2 hrs hills (1)
thursday	1 hr-1 hr 30 mins (1)	2-3 hrs hill reps or intervals (2)	30-45 mins easy (3)
friday		rest day	
saturday	45 mins-1 hr open water (1)	2 hrs (2)	1 hr-1 hr 30 mins (3)
sunday		3-4 hrs	(30-45 mins)
approx. time	4-6 hrs	10-15 hrs	6-7 hrs
approx. distance	10-20 km	300-400 km	80-100 km

Comments   (See 4, competitive triathlete - long distance)

cyclic training

In cyclic training the duration and/or intensity of training is increased weekly and step by step, with easy weeks interspersed in the programme. If done properly, cyclic training can bring you to peak performance. The total training is the combination of training frequency, duration and intensity which means that when we increase the intensity and/or duration of our training sessions we increase the total amount of training.

We can still use the in-season training programmes as a basic guideline except that duration and intensity of the sessions will vary from week to week. The intensity and duration of the sessions will be decreased in the easy weeks with a step-like increase in training schedules in the hard weeks.

Cyclic training has been tried successfully by top runners and cyclists. The great advantage of the system is that the body and mind will get some much-needed respite during the recovery week and, as a consequence, higher training levels can be achieved in the harder weeks.

A cyclic training programme requires careful planning, great discipline and pace control. Before embarking on such a programme sound basic conditioning is required as well as a high level of skill in the three disciplines. The programme can be monitored by timed interval sessions or time trials but this is not essential. Experienced athletes know through their own feelings the level they have attained and this is a reliable guide.

Timed interval sessions are easily done in the pool where conditions are uniform. But for cycling and running it is better to rely on subjective feelings. Awareness of the body signals such as breathing and muscle soreness are a reliable pace guide and should be observed in training.

Low priority races can be included in the harder weeks.

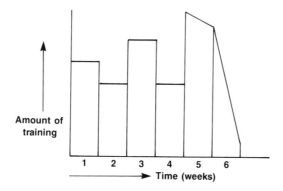

Fig. 1.

Outline of a 6-week training programme in a 2-week cycle - 1 hard week, 1 easy week.

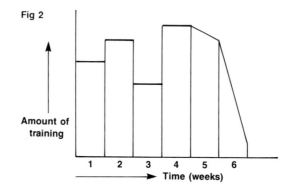

Fig. 2.

Outline of a 6-week training programme in a 3-week cycle - 2 hard weeks, 1 easy week.

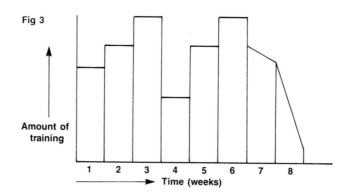

Fig. 3.

Outline of a 8-week trainin programme in a 4-week cycle - 3 hard weeks, 1 easy week.

There are many variations in which cyclic training can be applied (see Figs 1,2,3). The duration of the programme can be anywhere between four and twelve weeks preceding a race. It can be done for the three or two disciplines or only the one, with more conventional and steady training for the other two disciplines.

The following are examples of interval training sessions done in a hard week/easy week cycle.

swimming

(The times are approximate and are set only as an example.)

week 1: 4 x 400 m in 5.40 just below AT pace and 1-2 mins rest...hard week

week 2: 3-4 x 400 m in 5.45 with 1-2 mins rest...easy week

week 3: 5 x 400 m in 5.38 at AT pace with 1 min rest...hard week

week 4: 4 x 400 m in 5.42 with 1-2 mins rest...easy week

week 5: 5-6 x 400 m in 5.35 just above AT pace with 1/2-1 min rest...hard week

week 6: 6 x 200 m at AT pace with 1 min rest...tapering week

cycling

week 1: 2-4-6-4-2 mins repetitions at AT pace with 1 min easy pace in between...hard week

week 2: 4 x 2 mins repetitions at AT pace with 1 min easy in between...easy week

week 3: 2-4-6-6-4-2 mins repetitions at AT pace with 30 secs- 1 min easy pace in between...hard week

week 4: 5 x 2 mins repetitions at AT pace with 1 min easy in between...easy week

week 5: 4-6-8-6-4 mins repetitions just above AT pace with 30 secs easy pace in between...hard week

week 6: 4 x 2 mins repetitions at AT pace with 1 min easy in between...tapering

running

week 1: 4 x 1 mile intervals in 5.30 just below AT pace with 1-2 mins easy in between...hard week

week 2: 3-4 x 1 mile intervals in 5.35 with 1-2 mins easy in between...easy week

week 3: 5 x 1 mile intervals in 5.25 at AT pace with 1 min easy in between...hard week

week 4: 4 x 1 mile intervals in 5.30 with 1-2 mins easy in between...easy week

week 5: 5-6 x 1 mile intervals in 5.20 just above AT pace with 1 min easy in between...hard week

week 6: 6 x 200 m intervals at AT pace with 1 min in between...tapering
A similar session can be done away from a measured course as described for cycling with subjective feelings as a guide to monitoring levels of training.

Proper monitoring of subjective feelings will decide the success of this type of cyclic programme.

tapering and peaking

Tapering before an event will allow the body and the mind to recover from a period of heavy training. The cumulative effects of the harder training sessions will lead to the desired results but an accompanying feeling of tiredness, muscle soreness and sluggishness can not be avoided entirely. This tapering period can last anywhere from 2-10 days, depending on individual preference and the importance of the event. Tapering is done by decreasing duration of the workouts. A high intensity component is maintained with an emphasis on short time trials and a reduced amount of shorter repetitions at high intensity. Studies have shown that you can drop training duration by as much as 60-80% for two weeks without losing the edge. In fact, as long as a high intensity component is maintained an increased racing performance is a more likely result. The two days prior to the event consist of recovery sessions of shorter duration or, alternatively, complete rest.

If it is a low priority race (as part of a training programme leading up to a bigger race, to gain experience or to experiment with race pace and/or equipment) two days of recovery training is sufficient. The same counts for the recreational triathlete who is already training at a relatively easy pace. When you want to peak for a race, proper tapering is important and should include mental preparation. It is no use trying to peak, however, when training in the weeks or months leading up to the event has been interrupted or has not been done properly.

examples of a tapering programme before a low priority short distance triathlon

	swim	cycle	run
monday	1 hr-1 hr 30 mins	(1 hr)	1 hr-1 hr 30 mins plus intervals
tuesday	1 hr-1 hr 30 mins	2-4 hrs steady state	(15-30 mins)
wednesday	(1 hr)	1 hr 30 mins-2 hrs hills	1 hr hill reps
thursday	1 hr	1 hr 30 mins controlled intervals	
friday	30 mins	45 mins or total rest	
saturday	total rest		or 15-30 mins
sunday	race day		

Comments

*   Normal training is maintained up to two days before the event with an emphasis on slightly higher intensity and shorter duration of the training sessions.
*   The two days before the race can be spent resting (no training at all) or they can include some easy recovery sessions up to 45 mins in each discipline and no more than two disciplines per day.

examples of a tapering programme for a high priority short course triathlon

	swim	cycle	run
saturday	30-45 mins	1 hr-1 hr 15 mins	45 mins-1 hr steady state
sunday			1 hr 15 mins steady state or easy to steady pace with some controlled intervals
monday	30-45 mins	(45 mins-1 hr)	45 mins including 4 x 2 min intervals at AT pace
tuesday	30-45 mins	(2 hrs steady state)	(15-30 mins)
wednesday		1 hr-1hr 30 mins undulating ride	30-45 mins including strideouts
thursday	30 mins including controlled intervals	45 mins-1 hr including short sprints	
friday	15-30 mins easy including short sprints		30 mins easy including strideouts
saturday	rest day or easy ride 15-30 mins or run 15-30 mins		
sunday	race		

Comments

*   The taper starts eight days before the race with a decrease in the duration of the sessions.
*   On Monday and Tuesday the sessions are shorter but still contain interval work; shorter and fewer intervals of moderate or high intensity pace.
*   From Wednesday all workouts will be done at an easy to steady pace with some controlled intervals.
*   When in doubt, always choose an easier workout in the week before an event. Even four days without training will not result in a loss of fitness or form and will still enable you to peak.

examples of a tapering programme for a long distance triathlon.

	swim	cycle	run
saturday	45 mins	1 hr 30 mins	1 hr steady state
sunday			1 hr 30 mins
monday	1 hr 15 mins		1 hr 30 mins including submaximal intervals
tuesday	(30-45 mins)	2-3 hrs steady	
wednesday	45 mins easy		30 mins easy including strideouts
thursday	30 mins	1 hr with sprints	
friday	15-30 mins easy		15-30 mins easy
saturday		(30 mins easy)	
sunday	race day		

Comments

*   The duration of the sessions is reduced from 10 days before the event.
*   This programme is only advised for the more serious triathlete and should be accompanied by proper nutritional habits and mental attitude.
*   The last long run should be done approximately 12 days before the event and reduced in time, e.g. two hours rather than three hours.
*   The last long bike ride (3-4 hours) will be approximately 10 days before the event.
*   A high intensity component is maintained in most sessions till two days before the event.

post-race training

The feeling of euphoria and accomplishment following a race, especially when set goals have been reached or exceeded, urges many triathletes back into training the next day. On the day following an event you can feel surprisingly energetic which makes it even more tempting to complete a hard training session. The more experienced triathlete knows, however, that the feeling of tiredness, muscle soreness and even post-race depression does not set in fully until two or three days following the race. The harder you race the more obvious these symptoms are likely to be. They can be prolonged and even aggravated by a return to structured training when the body is not yet fully recovered.

A short distance event takes from 2-7 days to recover. For a long distance race it can be up to a month, or longer, if physical difficulties (heat exhaustion, dehydration) have been encountered during the race. The best way to recover is by rest (no training) or recovery training only, for as long as it takes.

specific development period (off-season training)

Most of the more serious triathletes train all year round with some professional triathletes having two subsequent competitive seasons - one in each hemisphere. These triathletes must ensure that they have at least six weeks' easy training between their competitive seasons. To maintain some basic fitness, three sessions a week per discipline will be sufficient. When starting your second season make sure you do at least 6 weeks of more specific training before you race. Follow the training programmes as suggested.

The majority of us, however, will look forward to the less pressured off-season during which time we can maintain fitness, improve on a weak discipline, enjoy our favourite discipline or even become involved in a completely different sport. For some, plain rest is tempting but not advised. It will take too much effort to regain fitness at the beginning of the next season and for any well-trained athlete it is just not healthy to stop all exercise completely. A feeling of being unwell and of rapid weight gain are two of the known withdrawal symptoms when athletes stop training abruptly and for a longer period of time. So, for health reasons, it is recommended to maintain at least some form of physical activity although this does not necessarily have to be related to the triathlon.

For the serious triathlete it is essential to use the off-season to improve the weakest discipline. The non-swimmer should join a swimming squad, the non-cyclist a cycling club and the runner a harrier club. By training with, and competing against, specialist swimmers, cyclists and runners, a rapid improvement can be achieved especially if there is some form of coaching involved.

The emphasis of training will be on duration and technique with interval training done at submaximal or moderate intensity pace. Strength training can also be incorporated into these sessions.

While specialising in one event during the winter months maintain some fitness in the other disciplines by doing easy workouts two or three times a week per discipline, if you have time and energy available.

The off-season is also a suitable time to do weight training to strengthen specific muscle groups. Again, results will be achieved only by regular workouts (at least three times a week and for a minimum of between six and eight weeks). If you live in an area where off-season weather conditions are harsh you can invest in a turbojet pool, a treadmill and an exercycle to maintain your triathlon fitness, and to overcome those long dark winter hours. The following programmes are for the more serious triathlete who wants to improve their weak discipline during the off-season.

off-season training programme for a non-swimmer

	swim	cycle	run
monday	1 hr-1 hr 30 mins	1 hr	
tuesday	1 hr-1 hr 30 mins		45 mins
wednesday		1 hr-1 hr 30 mins	
thursday	1 hr-1 hr 30 mins		45 mins
friday	(1 hr)		
saturday	1 hr		45 mins
sunday		1 hr 30 mins	

Comments

* If possible join a swimming squad.
* Do this programme continuously for 3-6 months and with proper coaching, improvement is guaranteed.
* The emphasis in the training will be on technique and duration with some interval work.
* The bike and run sessions can be missed but try not to miss any of your swimming sessions.
* Compete in swimming races if you wish, concentrating on freestyle events.
* Spend most of your time in freestyle training. Do not waste too much time on other strokes (use them mainly for warming up, recovery and flexibility).

off-season programme for a non-cyclist

	swim	cycle	run
monday		1 hr easy	30-45 mins
tuesday	30 mins	1 hr 30 mins-2 hrs including long intervals	
wednesday		2-3 hrs	
thursday	30 mins	1 hr 30 mins-2 hrs including time trial	
friday		rest day	
saturday		1 hr 30 mins	30-45 mins
sunday		4 hrs	

Comments

* Join a cycling club and experience the fun of bicycle racing. But, beware, most cyclists will be out to teach you a lesson, especially initially. Be a "defensive driver". Keep your eyes and ears open and you will learn much.
* Cyclists will teach you the art of spinning which can improve your cycling technique.
* Try and do your long ride with other cyclists.
* Training on a windload ergometer is an excellent form of strength training and can be done if the weather is bad or as a regular part of the training programme. Rollers have much less resistance; they will improve technique but not endurance or strength.
* The interval training can be done as repetitions, e.g., 4 x 2 mins to 4 x 8 mins or 2-4-6-8-6-4-2 mins etc., all with 1 min easy pace in between. Gradually build up the duration and intensity of the intervals and shorten the rest periods.
* The time trial can take anywhere between 20 mins and 50 mins. Use the same course so you can monitor improvement. Take weather conditions into account.
* The swim and run sessions are optional. An easy swim following a hard bike ride is great recovery.

off-season training programme for a non-runner

	swim	**cycle**	**run**
monday	30 mins	1 hr 30 mins	30 mins easy
tuesday			1 hr-1 hr 30 mins intervals
wednesday		1 hr	30 mins easy
thursday	30 mins		1 hr including sandhills or hill repetitions
friday		rest day	
saturday		1-2 hrs	1 hr steady state
sunday			1 hr 30 mins easy

Comments

* The hard/easy day principle should be applied strictly.
* The intervals can be done in the form of accelerations at AT pace, e.g., 4 x 2 mins; 1-2-3-4-4-3-2-1 mins; 2-4-6-4-2 mins; 5 x 3 mins etc., all with 1 minute easy jogging in between.
* If no hills are available try and find undulations, sandhills, steps or stairs. This type of strength training is a sure way to improve your running, especially at the end of that long hard bike ride.
* The long run on Sunday should be done at an easy pace.
* Compete in cross-country races and road races, and practise pacing yourself through a race.

* Train with other athletes if you can but make sure they are at a similar level to you.
* The swim and bike sessions are optional. An easy swim following a hard run enhances recovery.

off-season training programme for a triathlete aiming to run a marathon.

	swim	cycle	run
monday	30 mins	1 hr 30 mins	(30 mins)
tuesday			1 hr 30 mins including longer intervals e.g. 4 x 5 mins at AT pace
wednesday		1 hr	30 mins easy
thursday	30 mins		1 hr 30 mins steady state
friday		rest day	
saturday		1-2 hrs	1 hr steady state
sunday			2-3 hrs easy weekly or alternative weeks (with 1 hr-1 hr 30 mins other week)

Comments

* Ideal for triathletes who have a non-running background and who plan to do a full distance triathlon in the future.
* Most of the training will be done at easy or steady state pace.
* Interval sessions are optional.
* The long run should be built up gradually over time, increasing duration approximately 10-15 minutes every week or fortnight.
* When running takes longer than 1 hr carry fluids and practise drinking as fluids are essential during a marathon. Drinking during training will prevent dehydration and enhance recovery.
* Do this type of programme for at least 6-8 weeks with 2-3 long runs of which the duration should be close to the expected finishing time.
* Take approximately 10 days of tapering unless you do carbohydrate loading. In this case do a 1 hr 30 mins depletion run five days before the event at steady state followed by recovery sessions of short duration for the remaining days.
* The last long run should be done approximately two weeks before the marathon.
* Novice runners should not embark on this programme until they have developed a proper running base. This will take at least six months.

9

altitude training

While the scientists still argue about the pros and cons of altitude training, more and more triathletes are trying this method of training to improve performance.

The problem for scientists is to prove beyond reasonable doubt that altitude training is the prime reason for boosting performance. Some are still concerned that improvements measured are solely the result of a period of intense training in an environment away from home.

However, in general, and especially for the elite, experienced triathlete whose performance level has plateaued, altitude training is now considered a safe and effective training method. Although scientific literature gives a confusing picture, recent anecdotal information strongly favours this type of training.

The question now is not so much does it work, but how do you get the best results from altitude training. What is the best altitude to train at, do you adjust your training in any way and how long do you need to spend at altitude to get an optimum effect, are some of the questions that athletes want answered.

how does altitude training work?

The effects of altitude training are thought to be caused by the decreased oxygen level in the air at altitude. Less oxygen is bonded to the haemoglobin in the red blood cells and the body responds by increasing the haemoglobin and red cell production. This increases the oxygen-carrying capacity of the blood in a way which is comparable with blood doping or taking erythropoetin (**see Chapter 17, "Medical Matters"**).

The difference, however, is that the increase of haemoglobin and red blood cells is always within normal physiological limits, thereby avoiding increased blood viscosity which can be a side effect from the more artificial ways of enhancing red blood cell concentrations and which can have serious consequences.

Once the athlete returns from altitude to sea level there is an abundance of haemoglobin present to cope with the sudden increase in oxygen pressure in the air and a relative over-saturation of the blood with oxygen is the result. This, in turn, will support an efficient energy metabolism in the working muscle. A second effect from altitude training is a slower lactate response to submaximal exercise and possibly a shift of the anaerobic threshold to a higher exercise intensity when returning to sea level.

This can partly be explained by the increase in oxygen carrying capacity of the blood and additional changes which take place within the muscle cell when exposed to altitude training.

practical aspects of altitude training

Following are some practical aspects of altitude training based on the scientific and anecdotal evidence available, as well as recent experience of the author preparing for the 1992 World Championships at altitude.

* The most effective altitude at which to train seems to be 1500-2000 metres (5000-7000 feet), below which there are few measurable effects and above which it becomes too difficult to train hard.

* Three weeks is the minimum time needed to adjust to altitude training and acquire the benefits.

* The overall effects of altitude training last 1-3 weeks when coming down to sea level. The physiological effects (haemoglobin level in the blood, lactate threshold) are most pronounced in the first few days. This initial period following a return to sea level can be used for an important race (the sooner the better), or alternatively, for a period of heavy training from which the benefits will then be reaped at a later stage. The benefits and effects of altitude training are not maintained beyond this 1-3 week period.

* Athletes who have only limited time available at altitude gain more from altitude training if they have already reached a level of optimum fitness before going to altitude.

* Most athletes feel reasonably well in the first one or two days following arrival at altitude, except for a reduced training tolerance. This is often followed by a short period (one or two days) of excessive tiredness. This can be minimised by reducing training intensity and duration in those first few days allowing the body to adjust gradually.

* Most athletes find that following the initial "shock" period they can train at, or close to, similar training loads compared with sea level.

* Most triathletes find swimming the hardest to adjust to at altitude, followed by running and then cycling.

* The effects of altitude are mainly felt when doing harder workouts.

* Times for time trials and repetitions can be expected to be slightly slower for running and swimming than at sea level. In running this can be compensated for by doing faster workouts on a gradual down slope which allows for control of running intensity without sacrificing speed.

* The thin air decreases air resistance when cycling, contributing to higher speeds.

* Exposure to altitude in the initial stages contributes to dehydration due to hormonal influences. A reduction in plasma volume is the result and a subsequent impairment in performance. Careful attention, therefore, needs to be given to fluid replacement when training at altitude.

* Altitude training does not work equally for everyone. Athletes with a low initial haemoglobin level seem to respond best. Some athletes feel that altitude training affects their performance in a negative sense, or they are frequently ill. This is possibly because of inappropriate training programmes (too much, too little) or through training above the recommended altitude.

summary

The pendulum is swinging in favour of altitude training, depending on the level of altitude, allowance for gradual adjustment (with attention to dehydration) and use of proper training methods.

Scott Molina training at altitude in Colorado.

10 swimming

Swimming is by far the most complicated of the three disciplines to learn. That is why triathletes with a background in swimming have such an advantage as they have learned the proper swimming techniques at a young age when the body is more susceptible to acquiring new skills. Swimmers often make good triathletes.

Triathletes who take up swimming at a later age (over 18 years) will never be able to bridge the gap completely unless they have an exceptional talent for the sport. Athletes often become frustrated with the new sport because their improvement does not match their high expectations. They do not realise that to develop swimming skills takes time, patience and perseverance. You can become a good cyclist in a year but to become a competent swimmer can take three times as long.

It is essential, if you do not have a background in swimming, to receive professional coaching either privately or by joining a squad. Constant and accurate coaching on technique will speed the learning process. Do not expect immediate results, however, and be prepared to spend time on specific drills to improve your technique. In time results will come.

It helps to find a coach who knows about triathletes and triathlons; a coach who realises that triathletes differ from competitive swimmers in that they train solely for long distance freestyle swimming in open water while keeping in mind the other disciplines of cycling and running.

Naturally the great majority of training sessions will take place in a pool because of convenience and especially because a pool is superior to open water when it comes to quality training. During the season, however, it is advisable to have one open water swim a week **(see Chapter 8, "Training Programmes")** to familiarise oneself with rough water swimming, currents and navigation.

When training, do not waste too much time on the other strokes except when warming up and cooling down, and recovery in between repetitions. An exception, perhaps, is butterfly which is an excellent stroke for strength and fatigue training and, as the underwater stroke closely resembles the freestyle stroke, it will enhance freestyle performance. Do not spend too much time on kicking unless it is part of technique training.

Swimmers have the time to improve their kicking and sprinters will benefit from training with legs only, but triathletes have no extra time to spare and they will need their legs only for support and balance rather than propulsion. In contrast to kicking, swimming with arms only (with or without the use of buoyancy aids or extra drag) is a highly efficient and specific form of strength training but this should only be done if a proper freestyle technique has been mastered.

*   A word of caution on the use of hand paddles. They can contribute to one of the few serious swimming injuries - swimmers' shoulder. Opinions differ on the training benefits of hand paddles and they are best avoided by triathletes who have an inadequate technique or who have a tendency to develop shoulder pain.

Sprint repetitions of less than 200 metres are popular among swimmers but are less important to triathletes. They should only be done when perfecting technique and improving strength (interspersed with longer rests) or as endurance training with short rests (30 seconds or less).

There are two factors which determine performance in freestyle swimming, the distance covered per stroke (mainly related to technique) and the amount of work per stroke (related to power output). An increase in power output can be achieved by swimming with hand paddles, swimming with arms only and sprint swimming with long rest intervals. An improved technique and subsequent distance per stroke can be improved by one or two arm technique drills.

The following exercise will create an awareness of stroke development.

Swim a short distance (e.g. 25 m), note the time it takes and count the number of strokes. At each consecutive lap the sum of the time and number of strokes must be smaller.

When fatigue sets in, there is a decrease in propelling efficiency due to a loss of technique as well as power output.

In training, therefore, the emphasis should be on the importance of maintaining good technique when fatigue sets in as well as exercises which improve power output.

stroke technique

Although it is legal to use any stroke in a triathlon, most serious competitors use the freestyle or crawl. In Europe and Japan many recreational triathletes use breaststroke which is slower but easier for breathing and navigation.

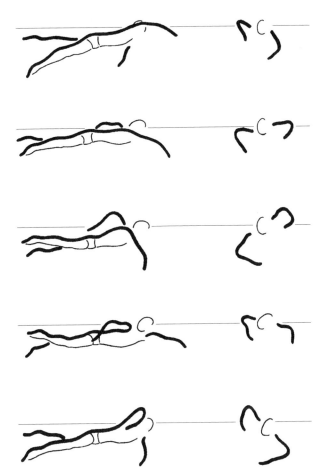

Fig. 1.

The 5 sections of the crawl : entry, catch, pull, follow-through and recovery

As many books have been written on swimming we will restrict ourselves to describing the basics of the freestyle technique, the fastest and most efficient of the different strokes for the purpose of triathlons.

body position
The position in the water should be horizontal with the head slightly lifted so that the water hits the hairline and you are looking halfway between forward and downward at an angle of 45 degrees.

the arm action
There are five parts of the arm action of the crawl: the entry, the catch, the pull, the follow-through and the recovery (see Fig. 1).

The entry: the hand enters the water with the arm not quite fully extended and slightly to the side of the body's mid-line. The hand enters the water thumb first so that it produces a smooth entry.

To practise the entry, swim with your head up so that you can see your hand enter the water. This can be done also by using one arm only, alternating arms after a half or full length of the pool. A pull buoy can be used between the legs and lower body.

Common errors: entering the hand too wide or across the mid-line (over-reaching) which will cause a sideways movement of the hip and make for a less effective pull.

Fig. 2.

The entry, catch, pull, follow-through as seen from underneath.

Entering the hand with a straight arm will cause a downward movement in the initial phase of the pull which causes raising of the shoulders and a subsequent vertical "bobbing" of the body.

Entering the hand too close to the head causes a catch which is too deep, and the loss of the initial portion of the pull.

The catch: after the hand has entered the water it is extended forward in a smooth manner and at a slightly downward angle until the arm is fully extended. At this stage there is a definite glide. At the end of the catch the hand will be 15-20 cm under the water surface with the wrist slightly flexed. The hand is cupped and the fingers are together, not allowing the water to slip through. The head is turned sideways in preparation for breathing.

The pull: this starts when the hand is flexed at the end of the catch and finishes when the arm is under the shoulder.

During the pull the elbow is gradually bent to an angle of 90-100 degrees by the time it reaches the end of the pull. For an efficient power output, the forearm is brought under the body with the hand touching but not crossing the mid-line.

Towards the end the working shoulder drops lower to provide strength and length to the stroke. This motion will also enhance a high elbow recovery for the opposite arm by causing the body to roll. At the end of the pull the opposite hand will start the entry.

A one-arm freestyle drill whereby the other arm is kept fully extended in front (with or without support of a kickboard) is an effective way of practising the pull. By wearing goggles you can follow the pattern of the pull exactly and critically. This drill can be done with or without the use of a pull buoy between the legs.

The follow-through: the follow-through is accomplished by extending the elbow gradually, when moving the hand past the hips. This movement is accelerated especially towards the point where the hand comes out of the water but without losing the feel of the water. At the end of the follow-through the palm is facing the thigh which will allow the hand to leave the water in a smooth and continuous motion.

A common error is for the hand to exit the water before the follow-through is completed. The follow-through can be practised also, with one-arm drills (with or without the use of a pull buoy) and with the emphasis on acceleration, especially towards the end of the action. To make sure the follow-through is complete you can touch your thigh with your thumb before the hand leaves the water. Another good way to check on a properly executed follow-through is to use hand paddles without a wrist strap. They tend to fall off if the hand is not pushed through fully at the end of the stroke.

The recovery: the elbow breaks through the water while the hand finishes the follow-through. During the recovery the elbow is kept higher than the hand when it is brought forward. The hand and forearm are as relaxed as possible while the hand is kept low over the water surface and close to the body. The high elbow position is made easier by the body-roll (mentioned in "the pull" section) and by turning the upper arm inwards. Arm recovery takes less time than the stroke under the water, resulting in one arm entering the water as the other is about halfway through its underwater stroke. The most common error is that of a low, straight-arm recovery, which results in a lateral motion of the hips and the crossing of the legs.

breathing

When the recovery hand enters the water the head is turned sideways towards the opposite side. Do not lift the head. The bow wave created by your head will cause a slight depression which will enable you to breathe lower than the actual water level.

While breathing in, you actually "look through" the recovery arm. Breathe in through your mouth. The face is turned back before the recovery hand enters the water. When executed properly the turning of the head will be incorporated with the body roll.

Immediately after turning your face back into the water, exhale steadily through the mouth and nose until the next breath. Failure to exhale sufficiently is a common mistake in learners.

You look through the recovery arm when breathing in.

It is wise to master the skill of bilateral breathing - breathing to alternate sides every three or five strokes. This balances the body's position in the water and makes it possible to swim in a straight line. It will also give you the option of breathing away from wind, waves and sun, or allow you to keep an eye on the competition and landmarks.

the kick

A vigorous kick requires much energy for little return as it contributes only 10-15 percent of the forward propulsion, presuming that the swimmer has a good kicking technique and is flexible in the ankles. Distance swimmers and triathletes obviously need to conserve energy and, therefore, the legs should only be used to stabilise the body.

Fig. 3.

At the end of the downbeat, the knee is almost straight and the foot is just below the level of the chest at its deepest point. The feet are pointed but relaxed during the upbeat.

The kick is divided into two movements - the downbeat and the upbeat.

The movement for the kick starts from the hip and goes via the knee, which is slightly bent (30-40 degrees) to the ankle and foot. On the downward beat the ankle will be straightened and the toes pointed as the top of the foot is pushed down through the water. At the end of the downbeat the knee is almost straight and the foot is just below the level of the chest at its deepest point.

During the upbeat the hip and knee are again leading. They start the upbeat just before the foot completes the downbeat. The feet are still pointed but relaxed during the upbeat.

A good kick boils the water without splashing. Kicking can be done in a cycle of 2, 4 or 6 beats per stroke (1 complete stroke is 2 arm strokes). A 2-beat kick is preferable as it is most efficient. The 4- and 6-beat kicks give more support for the slower swimmer and, if executed properly, contribute to the propulsion. The timing of the leg action should be allowed to occur naturally.

open water swimming

Open water swimming is different from pool swimming in that the water is usually cooler, there is no black line on the bottom to keep you on course and rough water can hamper breathing. In addition, currents and tides can sweep you off course. Taken all together, with the thought of jellyfish and sharks, there are enough reasons for many would-be triathletes to think twice before they enter the sport.

The only way to become familiar with open water swimming is practice. Safety is of paramount importance when training in open water, especially in the open sea, so never swim by yourself. Arrange for a canoe or row-boat escort, or swim with others. Even with these safeguards ask onlookers to keep a watchful eye on you in case of trouble.

If the water temperature is less than 16°C, forget about the swim; if it is less than 18°C a wetsuit and swimcap are strongly recommended to protect you from the effects of hypothermia. Good vision and navigation are of crucial importance in open water swimming. Goggles will assist vision.

Before getting into the water navigate the course you intend to swim by lining up with landmarks. Do not rely too much on buoys as you will be surprised how they diminish in size once you are in the water. They can even disappear completely if the water is rough. During the swim, line up the landmarks or buoys by doing a waterpolo stroke every 5-10 strokes. This means keeping your head out of the water with your chin on the surface for an entire stroke cycle. This requires an accentuated kick and so takes more energy. It pays to practise this stroke while training in the pool.

If there is a swell do your sighting on top of it. Take currents into account when navigating. When there is a side current aim "upstream" of the landmark, but how far you should go will depend on the strength of the current and your powers as a swimmer.

The advantages of bilateral breathing have been mentioned.

Breaking waves at the start of the swim can be conquered by the "dolphin" technique. This means diving underneath the wave just before it breaks on you, touching the bottom with your hands and pushing off with your legs. When completed, the wave will have passed. Dolphin out as far as you can before you start swimming, usually when the water is about hip deep.

In the triathlon, drafting during the swim is legal and it can save a considerable amount of energy. (Drafting is done by staying close to and in the same path as the swimmer ahead.) Try drafting in training. It is made easier by wearing a wetsuit which aids buoyancy.

swimming aids

The most significant legal aid to enhance performance is the wetsuit. A wetsuit increases buoyancy and speed because of less drag. It also helps to keep the body warm, prevents hypothermia and makes the swim/bike transition easier. On average, between one and two minutes can be saved in a 1500 metre swim by wearing a wetsuit. Improvement depends on the standard of swimming (slower swimmers benefit more) and the quality of the wetsuit. The smoother the surface the wetsuit has, the less drag, and the more buoyancy.

In recent years rapid improvements in design and materials have been made to the despair of the more serious and less financial triathletes.

For the recreational triathlete a wetsuit is not essential but it will assist comfort and definitely help prevent hypothermia which is always a risk if the water is below 18°C. A wetsuit needs to fit snugly for optimum buoyancy.

Goggles are now used by most triathletes and swimmers. In the pool they prevent the eyes from becoming irritated by chlorine and they improve underwater vision, and are good for stroke correction and avoiding collisions. In open water they contribute to overall vision and in sea water they protect the eyes from salt.

To prevent goggles from fogging up, spit in them then rinse them lightly with water before putting them on. If they leak re-adjust the fit. There are many shapes and sizes available so make sure you select a pair that best fits the contour of your face. For triathletes who wear glasses, consider purchasing prescription goggles.

A swimming cap improves speed by reducing drag. This is because the surface of the cap is so much smoother than hair. A cap will also help prevent hypothermia as heat loss through the head can be considerable (about 30 percent of all heat loss). In water less than 16°C two caps or a neoprene cap can be worn.

Pull buoys, a pair of foam cylinders attached together with a rope, are used for swimming with arms only and can be used when doing one-arm drills. The pull buoy is placed between the thighs and locked in place by squeezing the legs together. Kickboards can also be used to support the extended arm in front of the swimmer when practising one-arm drills. The technique can be practised with or without the use of a kickboard. The use of hand paddles was covered at the beginning of this chapter.

A wetsuit is a must for the competitive triathlete and when the water is cold.

11

cycling

Cycling is probably the most exciting of the three disciplines as there is a dependence on equipment and the generation of far greater speed compared with either swimming or running. This immediately adds an element of danger. This, however, does not seem to deter would-be triathletes from tackling the sport. Approximately 50 percent of triathletes have a background in running and most of these take to cycling easily.

Steve Gurney, champion multi-sport athlete on a new generation Pearson-designed composite frame. Note also the super-light, aerodynamic composite wheels.

Runners often do not make great swimmers but they can become good cyclists in a relatively short time. As runners are often individualists it is not surprising that they thrive on time-trialling - an aspect of cycling which many cyclists dislike. This is not to say that we cannot learn from the "pure cyclists". In fact, the only way to acquire bike handling skills, to learn about gears, equipment and repairs, is to join a cycling club and do some road racing.

This will give you an introduction to the sport quickly, with only slight adjustments having to be made to become a competent time trialist: lower the handlebars a fraction, use the aero handlebars; sit slightly more forward; forget about spinning and be prepared to use bigger gears; and last but most importantly, pay attention to aerodynamic effects.

Become an individualist again. Be prepared to hurt and you will leave many of the "pure cyclists" in your time-trialling wake.

cycling technique

The technique of pedalling mechanics and pedal cadence is probably the cyclist's greatest concern. Cycling, however, does not differ from other sports in the sense that many successful athletes have apparently non-optimal styles. It has, for example, been found that some elite cyclists generate large negative forces during the recovery (pull) phase of the pedalling action and critics will quickly point out that these cyclists could perform better with a more optimal riding style. Although the aim should be to try and continually improve technique, room should be left for the (tri) athlete to adapt to his or her own anatomical and physiological characteristics.

Many questions on the optimal pedalling technique in cycling are still unanswered.

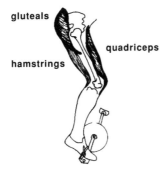

gluteals

quadriceps

hamstrings

Fig. 1.

The three main muscle groups involved in cycling - quadriceps, hamstrings and gluteals.

Biomechanically, the circular motion is more efficient than the up and down motion as the three main muscle groups involved in the cycling motion, gluteals (buttocks), quadriceps (front thigh) and hamstrings (rear thigh), work collectively (Fig. 1). This means that the basic principle in pedalling mechanics is to develop a smooth circular motion with even pressure applied throughout a large part of the pedalling circle. Studies have shown that in steady state cycling most of the force resulting in forward motion of the bike is created by the downward motion of the pedalling action (Fig. 2).

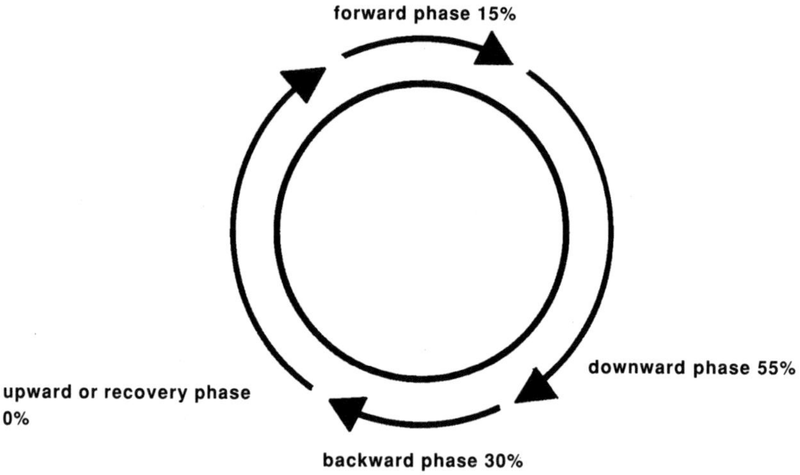

forward phase 15%

downward phase 55%

upward or recovery phase
0%

backward phase 30%

Fig. 2.

Approximate contributions
of forces during the different
cycles in the pedalling
action.

Although most cyclists will say they definitely pull up in the recovery phase, we
know now that the "pull up" usually results in no more than overcoming the weight
of gravity. This is contrary to the popular opinion that pulling up on the pedal can
result in a great improvement in efficiency. It has been confirmed that even elite
cyclists do no more than unload the pedal when involved in the "pull up" phase
during steady state cycling. But, during hill climbing and sprinting, real upward
forces can be applied in the recovery phase.

At present it seems that the technique should be aimed at a circular pedalling
action which maximises the propulsive effect of the downward phase and
eliminates the negative effective forces during the recovery phase. Within that
framework all riders will develop their own pedalling style which differs slightly in
force application from other riders. (See also Figs. 3 & 4.)

ankling
One of the indications of a proper pedalling action is the position of the foot during
the pedal revolution. Although no ideal pattern of ankling has been identified,
studies of the elite cyclists show that they have their toes pointing down for most of
the time. The higher the pedalling rate, the more the toes point downwards.

In general, when using lower pedalling rates (climbing or time-trialling) the foot will
point toward the horizontal or the toes will be slightly upward on the downward
phase of the pedalling action. Again, room should be left for individual preference.

pedal cadence
Pedal cadence refers to the number of pedal revolutions (cycles) completed per
minute (rpm).

For many years it has been considered by racing cyclists that a cadence or 90-100
rpm is the most efficient pedalling rate for steady state riding, but recent research
suggests that this is not the case. There is now evidence that maximum efficiency
is obtained at 60-90 rpm, also for prolonged periods of effort, with 80 rpm providing
the most efficient work rate.

Test results indicate that there are relatively larger negative effective force combinations during the recovery phase at higher rpms, so that the faster the riders spin, the more they work against themselves during recovery.

The cadence is decided by the gears we use. Gearing is decided by the size of the chain wheel (front), the size of the sprocket (back), the length of the crank and the diameter of the drive wheel. Generally, the recommended standard gear range is 52 or 53/42 x 13, 14, 15, 17, 19, 21 (referring to the numbers of teeth on the chain wheel and sprocket). Theoretically, this gives 12 different combinations but a couple (53-21 and 42-13) are lost through bad chain lines.

Fig. 3.
Foot position at low pedalling rate (60-80 rpm). On climbs and time trials the toes are tilted at the top dead centre and dropped at the bottom dead centre.

Fig. 4.
Foot position at higher pedalling rate (80-100 rpm) during training and when riding in bunches. The toes are dropped slightly during phase 1.

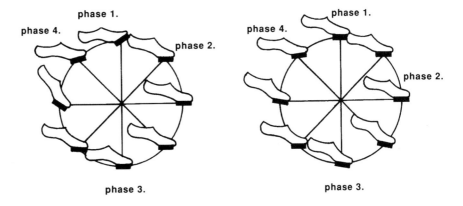

The following progression is from the lowest to the highest gear.

chainwheel		sprocket	
42	x	21	both used on steep hills.
42	x	19	
42	x	17	used on hills and with strong headwinds.
42	x	15	can be used for technique training (spinning), it is virtually the same as 52/53 x 19 but has a better chain-line.
42	x	14	has a better chain-line than 52/53 x 17 and should be used in preference.
52 or 53	x	19	
52 or 53	x	17	all four are used on the flat in training and racing.
52 or 53	x	15	
52 or 53	x	14	
52 or 53	x	13	used on downhills to gain or maintain momentum and with tailwinds on the flat.

Comments

* For very steep hills the 21 on the back might need to be replaced by a 23 or a 25.
* The diameter of a conventional racing wheel is 27 inches (68.58 cms). "Funny" time trial bikes often have a conventional sized rear wheel (27 inch) and a smaller front wheel (26 or 24 inch).
* The gear ratio is the gear in inches and is calculated as follows: number of teeth on the chain wheel multiplied by the diameter of the chain wheel in inches (27) divided by the number of teeth on the sprocket. For example, if you have a chain wheel with 53 teeth and a rear sprocket of 14, then you have a gear ratio of:

$$\frac{53 \times 27}{14} = 102.2 \text{ inches.}$$

In France the gear ratio is measured in metres and gives the distance travelled with one pedal revolution. Although not internationally used much, this method is more logical.

Gear (in metres) = number of teeth on the chain wheel multiplied by the circumference of the rear wheel (2.15 m) divided by the number of teeth on the rear sprocket.

Table 1   **summary of gear ratios**

sprocket   chainwheel   gear table in inches

teeth	42	43	44	45	46	47	48	49	50	51	52	53	54	55	56
12	94.5	96.8	99.0	101.3	103.5	105.8	108.0	110.3	112.5	114.8	117.0	119.3	121.5	123.8	126.0
13	87.2	89.3	91.4	93.4	95.4	97.5	98.8	101.8	103.8	105.8	108.1	110.0	112.1	114.2	116.3
14	81.0	82.9	84.9	86.8	88.7	90.6	92.5	94.5	96.4	98.4	100.3	102.2	104.2	106.0	107.3
15	75.6	77.4	79.2	81.0	82.8	84.6	86.4	88.2	90.0	91.8	93.6	95.4	97.2	99.0	100.8
16	70.9	72.5	74.3	76.0	77.6	79.3	81.0	82.7	84.4	86.1	87.8	89.5	91.2	92.8	94.5
17	66.7	68.3	69.9	71.5	73.0	74.6	76.2	77.8	79.4	81.0	82.6	84.2	85.6	87.3	88.9
18	63.0	64.5	66.0	67.5	69.0	70.5	72.0	73.5	75.0	76.5	78.0	79.5	81.0	82.5	84.0
19	59.7	61.1	62.5	64.0	65.4	66.8	68.2	69.6	71.1	72.5	73.9	75.4	76.7	78.0	79.4
20	56.7	58.1	59.4	60.8	62.1	63.5	64.8	66.2	67.5	68.9	70.2	71.6	72.8	74.2	75.6
21	54.0	55.3	56.6	57.9	59.1	60.4	61.7	63.0	64.3	65.6	66.9	68.1	69.4	70.5	72.0
22	51.5	52.8	54.0	55.2	56.5	57.7	58.9	60.1	61.4	62.6	63.8	65.0	66.3	67.5	68.7
23	49.3	50.5	51.7	52.8	54.0	55.2	56.3	57.5	58.7	59.9	61.0	62.2	63.3	64.5	65.7
24	47.3	48.4	49.5	50.6	51.8	52.9	54.0	55.1	56.3	57.4	58.5	59.2	60.0	61.8	63.0
25	45.4	46.4	47.5	48.6	49.7	50.8	51.8	52.9	54.0	55.1	56.2	57.4	58.3	59.4	60.4
26	43.6	44.6	45.7	46.7	47.8	48.8	49.8	50.9	51.9	52.9	54.0	55.0	56.1	57.1	58.1

sprocket	chainwheel													gear table in metres
teeth	42	43	44	45	46	47	48	49	50	51	52	53	54	55	56
12	7.47	7.65	7.83	8.01	8.18	8.36	8.54	8.72	8.90	9.07	9.25	9.43	9.61	9.79	9.97
13	6.90	7.06	7.23	7.39	7.55	7.72	7.88	8.05	8.21	8.38	8.54	8.70	8.87	9.03	9.20
14	6.40	6.56	6.71	6.86	7.01	7.17	7.32	7.47	7.63	7.78	7.93	8.08	8.23	8.39	8.54
15	5.98	6.12	6.26	6.40	6.55	6.69	6.83	6.97	7.12	7.26	7.40	7.54	7.69	7.83	7.97
16	5.60	5.74	5.87	6.00	6.14	6.27	6.40	6.54	6.67	6.81	6.94	7.07	7.20	7.34	7.47
17	5.27	5.40	5.52	5.65	5.78	5.90	6.03	6.15	6.28	6.40	6.53	6.66	6.78	6.91	7.03
18	4.98	5.10	5.22	5.34	5.45	5.57	5.69	5.81	5.93	6.05	6.17	6.29	6.40	6.52	6.64
19	4.72	4.83	4.94	5.05	5.17	5.28	5.39	5.50	5.62	5.73	5.84	5.95	6.07	6.18	6.29
20	4.48	4.59	4.70	4.80	4.91	5.02	5.12	5.23	5.34	5.44	5.55	5.66	5.76	5.87	5.98
21	4.27	4.37	4.47	4.57	4.67	4.78	4.88	4.98	5.08	5.18	5.29	5.39	5.49	5.59	5.69
22	4.07	4.17	4.27	4.37	4.46	4.56	4.66	4.75	4.85	4.95	5.04	5.14	5.24	5.34	5.43
23	3.90	3.99	4.08	4.18	4.27	4.36	4.45	4.55	4.64	4.73	4.83	4.92	5.01	5.10	5.20
24	3.73	3.82	3.91	4.00	4.09	4.18	4.27	4.36	4.45	4.54	4.62	4.71	4.80	4.89	4.98
25	3.58	3.67	3.76	3.84	3.93	4.01	4.10	4.18	4.27	4.35	4.44	4.52	4.61	4.69	4.78
26	3.45	3.53	3.61	3.69	3.78	3.86	3.94	4.02	4.10	4.19	4.27	4.35	4.43	4.51	4.60

body position

The three resisting forces to overcome when cycling are rolling resistance, wind resistance and when climbing, gravity.

On the flat wind resistance is the greatest force to overcome and as the human body has far higher wind resistance than the bicycle itself (70 versus 30 percent), improving your riding position is one of the most effective ways of increasing potential speed.

The greatest rolling resistance is caused by contact between the tyre tread and the road surface. Rolling resistance can be reduced by lowering the combined weight of rider and machine and using light, high pressure tyres. Friction of the turning pedals, friction of the bottom bracket bearings, friction of the chain, and friction of the wheel bearings all contribute to the rolling resistance. This can be minimised by using quality equipment and proper bike care.

Wind resistance can be reduced by a low (horizontal) upper body position with the hands on the drops and the elbows slightly bent, thereby reducing the frontal area of the machine and rider. A low position reduces wind resistance by half, compared with the upright leisure riding position.

Improving the shape of the cyclist by adopting an aerodynamic posture, smooth racing clothing (lying as close to the body as possible) and a smooth and stylish riding style improves the streamlining and, therefore, reduces the resistance even further. The biggest improvement in aerodynamics related to cycling has come from the introduction of the aerobars which decrease frontal resistance dramatically.

To feel comfortable in the aerodynamic position it needs to be practised, so make an effort to do 70-80 percent of your training in the racing position and it will become second nature when racing.

climbing

When riding on the flat only wind resistance and rolling resistance need be overcome but when climbing hills there is the additional resistance of gravity. Because of the considerably slower speeds and so much less wind resistance, a more comfortable (less aerodynamic) posture can be assumed. More oxygen is required in uphill cycling and a more upright position with hands on the brakehoods or on top of the bars allows for easier breathing.

Climbing can be done sitting or standing depending on the grade, the length of the climb and individual preference. For longer climbs it is a good idea to alternate sitting and standing as muscle groups used in both positions are slightly different. In this way extra use of specific muscle groups is prevented.

Shifting the body weight will cause the bike to rock. This motion is called "honking".

When standing, the full body weight can assist in the downward force of the pedalling action by shifting the centre of gravity directly over the pedal. Shifting the body weight to the other pedal will be accompanied by a tilting of the bike to the other side. This rocking motion is called "honking" by cyclists. Additional pulling upward on the recovery pedal allows for a more continuous power delivery.

Avoid excessive rocking by keeping your head inside the vertical plane made by the brakehoods. Do not lean too far over the front of the bike (by avoiding looking down and over the point of the front hub) when standing, as the rear wheel can lose grip and spin. Leaning too far back will prevent you using your body weight properly.

The upper body and upper extremities play a far greater role in climbing than when cycling on the flat. When sitting, the hands are usually on the brakehoods or on the tops. When standing, they can be either on the drops or on the brakehoods. Upper body strength is applied by pulling back and up on the bars or brakehoods while pushing down with the legs. Good upper body control will also guarantee that the tyres follow a straight line up the hill. Generally, a gearing that allows the cadence to stay between 60 and 80 will be acceptable for efficient power production in an uphill ride. Gearing selection is dependent on the rider's strength and the severity of the hill. When climbing, more power can be applied to the pedal by lowering your heel slightly in the down phase.

Uphill cycling is as much a psychological as a physical challenge. Practising uphill cycling will not only improve strength and speed but also mental toughness which is of crucial importance when racing.

descending

On some longer descents speeds of 80 km/h or more can be reached. Although going downhill at full speed can be an exhilarating experience, there is no doubt

Going downhill at full speed can be an exhilarating experience.

that crashing when doing so is the one fear most cyclists as well as triathletes have in common. Loose stones, a puncture or a stray dog can have dramatic consequences. With skill, however, and a bike in good mechanical condition, a lot of potential problems can be prevented.

At the start of a downhill section use a high gear to gain momentum until the legs start spinning. An aerodynamic position on the bike when descending is of crucial importance to obtain maximum speed. If the road surface is smooth and you are confident in your descent, having your hands on top of the bars will assist aerodynamically but for maximum control the hands are best on the drops with one or two fingers on the brakes. Keep your elbows tucked in and your knees close to the frame. The cranks and your feet should be in a horizontal position. Most of the weight should be on the pedals to lower the centre of gravity and increase stability and shock absorption. The leg muscles need to be kept as loose and relaxed as possible to prevent cramp and to get the maximum benefit from this "recovery period".

The much-dreaded speed wobble, a wild vibration of the bike, is caused by an improper weight distribution and can be counteracted by shifting weight, usually backwards.

cornering

When cornering the inside pedal is pulled up to prevent it touching the ground while the weight should be as much as possible on the outside pedal. By leaning bike and body weight into the bend, at the same time positioning the inner knee towards the apex of the bend, you can counter the tendency to drift out (Fig. 5). If you have to brake, do it before the bend, not while cornering. Braking at high speeds should be done gently and with a front-rear wheel ratio of approximately 60-40.

Fig. 5.

When cornering, the inside pedal is pulled up to prevent it touching the ground, while the weight remains as much as possible on the outside pedal.

The best line for cornering is to go as wide as possible (but stay on your half of the road) when entering the corner, hitting the apex on the inside of the corner and exiting as widely as possible. This lessens the radius of the bend and therefore reduces the forces which tend to pull the rider towards the outside (Fig. 6). If you are less confident or not fully familiar with the bend, middle cornering is safer leaving you with more room in case of unexpected tightening, loose gravel or potholes. Remember that the tendency to drift when cornering works mainly on the tyres so make sure that they are glued on properly.

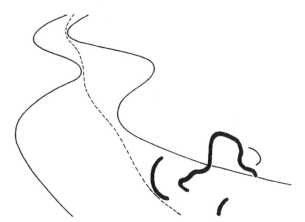

Fig. 6.

The best line for cornering is to go as wide as possible when entering the corner, hitting the apex on the inside of the corner and exiting as widely as possible.

the bike

The development and design of bikes is progressing so fast that revolutionary new ideas become dated quickly. Helped by new materials available and aided by an increased awareness of the importance of aerodynamics, new designs in frames, wheels and other bike equipment appear on the market almost monthly. Disc wheels and "funny bikes" are recognised as having advantages under certain conditions, while aero handlebars also give a clear edge.

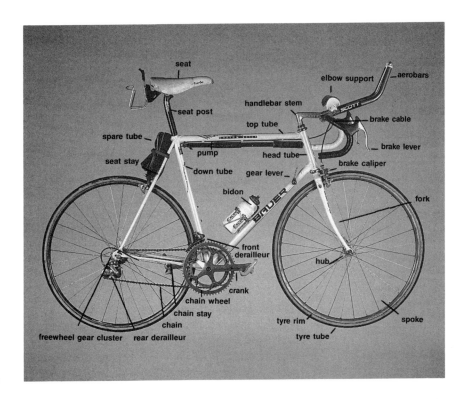

A triathlete's cycle, complete with accessories.

As long as no rules are introduced regulating the nature of bicycle equipment, the search for the ultimate bike will go on much to the despair of the more serious triathlete who is short of cash but keen to explore avenues which can give an advantage when racing. It must be remembered, however, that fancy equipment can never make up for a deficient training schedule. It will always be your legs you will have to rely on most.

frame size and material

Choosing the right frame size is the first step towards achieving proper body positioning on the bike. The best equipment is useless if the frame is too big or too small.

The initial measurement for the frame is its basic size measured from the centre of the bottom bracket shell to the top of the seat lug. Some manufacturers measure the frame from the centre of the bottom bracket shell to the centreline of the top tube.

You can work out your frame size from your inside leg measurement. In bare feet measure your leg length from the floor to the crutch. Subtract 10 inches or 25 cm to get your approximate frame size. In cases of doubt go for a frame slightly smaller rather than bigger.

The great majority of triathletes will find that a factory frame is an excellent fit. Individual adjustments can then be made by altering stem length, seat height and position. People who vary greatly from the norm in size (a good indication for this is if you have difficulty getting clothes) might require a custom-made frame.

An important measure for the more serious triathlete who is using aerobars is the seat tube angle. This is the angle between the seat tube and the top tube. In conventional frames this angle is usually between 72 and 74°. By having an angle of 76-80° the position of the seat will be further forward. This allows the angle between the torso and the thighs to open up which is especially important when using aerobars. As a consequence you get more leverage from the quadriceps muscles and restricted wheeling. Some factory frames are now produced which have a steeper seat tube angle. Alternatively, a custom-made frame can offer the solution. Most competitive triathletes agree that a seat tube angle of 78-80° is optimal with the front of the seat approximately level with the crankset.

Once you have found your frame size you can choose from frames made of different materials. The most important features are lightness and stiffness. The stiffer the frame the more energy is transferred to the pedals. Lightness is especially advantageous on a hilly course but a lighter machine is pointless if the rider is overweight.

Carbon fibre frames are continuing to evolve and are now superior in their lightness and stiffness compared with steel and aluminium. But they are still rather expensive. Standard diameter aluminium frames are lighter but slightly more flexible than steel frames and they fatigue in time, losing responsiveness. The bigger size frames (56 cm), show increased flexibility which might compromise on performance. They can contribute to the dreaded speed wobble during high speed descents. Oversize (large diameter tubing) aluminium models, however, are stiffer than the standard diameter frames and they are a reliable and cost-effective alternative to steel.

In making your frame choice, consider your size, your goals, level of experience and personal riding style. For most triathletes a conventional, good quality, steel frame will still be a competitive, reliable and durable choice.

Once you have found the right frame size, further adjustments to proper positioning on the bike can be made with the following guidelines.

Everybody differs in body proportions and riding style. Be prepared to experiment taking the neutral position as a starting point.

seat height
Proper seat height and position will help to obtain maximum efficiency from your leg muscles while cycling. The seat height is the distance measured from the bottom bracket axle to the theoretical point where the extended seat tube meets the surface of the seat.

A more practical way of establishing seat height is by setting the pedals in the vertical position and then placing your heel on the lower pedal. The leg in this position should be straight.

seat position
Seat position can be corrected by forward and backward movement. In the neutral position the front of the seat should be between 1 cm and 5 cm behind a line falling through the bottom bracket axle. When using aerobars in general, the seat needs to be placed slightly up and further forward with the front of the seat touching the imaginary vertical line drawn through the centre of the bottom bracket. This can be achieved by using a special (bend) seatpost or a specially designed frame with a steeper seat tube angle as explained before. Seat position depends a great deal on riding style and individual preference. The more technical rider will tend to sit toward the back while the power cyclist (which many triathletes are) tends to prefer a more forward position.

seat inclination
The neutral position is horizontal. The seat nose can be tilted slightly upwards if you have the tendency to slide forwards. Women often find it more comfortable to have their seat nose tilted slightly down.

reach
The reach is measured from the back of the seat to the start of the handlebars. In the neutral position the reach should be the same as the seat height. The reach can be adjusted by changing the length of the stem. When sitting on the bike in racing position, with the hands on the drops and the cranks parallel to the down tube, the upper knee should just overlap the elbow.

When using aerobars the forward position of the seat can be compensated for by using a longer stem.

handlebar height
The tops of conventional handlebars and the elbowpads of aerobars should be 1-5 cm below the seat. If the handlebars are too high the aerodynamic position is lost more easily. If too low, it can hamper breathing. People with longer arms can have their bars a little lower. Have your handlebars as low as comfort will allow to gain optimum advantage of an aerodynamic position.

aerobars
Aerobars come in many different shapes and sizes. The clip on models which, as the name says, clip on to conventional handlebars, are most popular.

Most important is that they are stiff and not too heavy. It is also good if the elbowpads can be placed at different widths.

The closer they are together, the better the aerodynamic effect. However, comfort is also important and athletes with wider and stiffer shoulders need to take that into consideration.

The length of the aerobars depends on the length of the forearm. Again, personal preference comes in, along with seat position in relation to arm position.

crank length
The most commonly used sizes in crank length are 170 mm, 172.5 mm and 175 mm. Standard bikes are usually sold with 170 mm cranks. As cranks get larger, leverage increases and more power can be applied.

Research indicates that if you outfit your bike with cranks 2.5 mm longer and a chain ring that is 1 tooth larger (53 instead of 52), the larger cranks will allow you to turn the 53 as if it were a 52. The more serious triathlete should, therefore, use 172.5 mm (for the small to average build) or 175 cm for the larger build. Some of the top triathletes will go for 180 mm.

handlebar width
The width of the handlebars should correspond with the width of the shoulders. A 40 cm width will suit the majority of triathletes. Once you have your bike sized put the essential measurements down in a diagram.

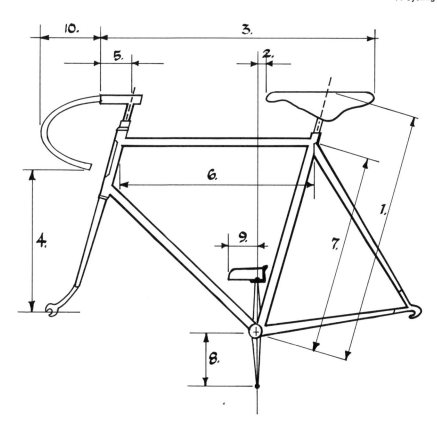

Fig. 7.
Write down your bike
measurements for future
reference.

1) Seat height .... cm
2) Seat position .... cm
3) Reach .... cm
4) Handlebar height .... cm
5) Stem length .... cm
6) Top tube length .... cm
7) Frame size .... cm
8) Crank length .... cm
9) Toe clip length .... cm
10) Handlebar forward throw .... cm

Some guidelines on measurement are given below.

Table 2.	tall build	medium build	small build
frame size	58-60 cm	55-58 cm	51-55 cm
handlebar width	40-41 cm	39-40 cm	38-39 cm
stem length	11-13 cm	10-12 cm	8-10 cm
crank length	172.5-175 mm	170-175 mm	170-172.5 mm

wheels and tyres

The most effective means of increasing your bicycle's potential performance is by way of a lightweight pair of wheels. Most serious triathletes now use disc wheels or, at least, aerodynamically spoked and rimmed wheels for racing.

Disc wheels are now of similar weight to the many conventional wheels and can, therefore, also be used on a hilly course. In the last few years there has been a tremendous interest in the development of one-piece, lightweight, composite (carbon/Kevlar) wheels with few (3-8) spokes. The Hed disc wheels and aerodynamically built spoked CX wheels have been in the forefront of wheel development using extensive wind tunnel testing to measure aerodynamic advantage.

Scientists are still searching for the optimal combination of aerodynamics, stiffness, strength and lightness but it is likely that sooner rather than later composite wheels will become more easily available and affordable. Tubular tyres (also called singles or sewn ups) are no longer superior in performance to clinchers (which have a separate tube inside) as clincher technology has improved dramatically. The most important advantage of a tubular tyre is the speed with which it can be changed when you get a puncture during a race. A spare tube can be folded and conveniently carried under the seat. In general, tubulars puncture more easily than clinchers and are more expensive to use so the recreational triathlete is better off with conventional wheels and the use of clinchers for training and racing. Ideally, the more serious triathlete should have a pair of training wheels with clinchers or sturdier tubulars and a set of racing wheels as aerodynamically built as cost allows. Some triathletes have a training bike and a racing bike. During racing, tyre pressure should be 90-110 p.s.i. High quality racing tyres can be pumped up to 140-160 p.s.i.

There is continuing research for lighter, stronger, more reliable and more aerodynamically shaped cycling components, just as there is for frames and wheels.

pedals

Pedals vary in weight, design, price and the type of bearings used. Pedals with toe clips have almost become obsolete for the serious triathlete since the introduction of the quick-release pedals pioneered by Look. The biggest advantage of quick-release pedals, besides comfort, is that they shorten the transition time which is so important in short distance events.

Recreational triathletes can use conventional pedals with or without toe clips and with a choice of running shoes or the generally better performing cycling shoes.

The crankset consists of the crankarms (to which the pedals attach), chainrings, bearings and cups, and the spindle.

The spindle, bearings and cups that fit into the bottom bracket shell on the frame, make up the bottom bracket. The bottom bracket must match the crankset and the threads that are cut into the frame's bottom bracket shell. Sizes may vary depending on where the frame and the components are manufactured.

The front and rear derailleurs are responsible for sliding the chain between the chainrings at the front and the cogs at the rear. Both derailleurs need to be compatible with the crankset and the freewheel, and need to be properly adjusted. Shimano introduced the revolutionary index-shifter in 1985. With standard derailleurs you have to overshift a little to get the chosen gear and then adjust the shift levers back slightly for proper positioning of the chain. With the index-shifter the derailleur goes into the right gears automatically and exactly. On undulating or hilly terrain in particular, where gears need to be changed frequently, this can be an advantage. Derailleurs can be moved by adjusting screws which determine how far the derailleur can go from side to side.

Gearing has been discussed under pedal cadence and is decided by the number of teeth on the front chainring and the rear sprocket (also called a freewheel or cog). The standard chainrings are 42/52 or 53 and a sprocket with 13, 14, 15, 17, 19, 21 tooth cogs will be suitable for most courses.

Steep, long hill climbs can be handled by adding a larger gear to the freewheel or by putting a smaller chainring in the front. Large gentle downhill sections as well as a strong tailwind can be handled by the use of a smaller sprocket (12) at the rear and a large (53 or 54) chainwheel at the front.

Freewheels require special tools for removal and this is best done by a cycle mechanic.

brakes

Tests have shown that aero brake levers are just as sensitive and effective as standard levers and they do give a significant aerodynamic advantage.

Brakes have either a side pull or a centre pull mechanism. The side pull brakes have more braking power and are preferred by most cyclists and triathletes. Good brakes have a quick release system which increases the distance between the brake blocks. This allows for an easier wheel change. An added advantage is that when a spoke breaks and the wheel buckles, you can continue without the rim rubbing against the brake blocks.

The brake levers should be positioned so that it is easy to operate them from the top and from the drops. The blocks and brakes should be adjusted properly, preferably by an experienced mechanic. When the brakes are full on the lever should not touch the handlebars. No money should be saved on a set of reliable and smooth working brakes as there might come a time when your life will depend on them.

shoes and clothing

Proper cycling shoes will contribute to a smoother and more economic cycling action and are a must for the serious triathlete, especially in hilly terrain. They must have a rigid sole and fit the foot snugly with ample room to manoeuvre the toes to prevent cramp. The cleat is properly adjusted when the ball of the foot is directly over the pedal axle and the inside heel of the foot clears the crank arm by about 1 cm.

Cycling shorts which have padding in the crutch are more comfortable, while cycling shirts also have pockets in the back which are handy for carrying food, tools and money. Cycling gloves increase riding comfort and they will protect the hands in a crash. They can also be used to clean the tyres of road glass and gravel while in motion.

An approved cycling helmet is must for training and racing.

aerodynamic advantages

Aerodynamic handlebars improve your "shape" on the bike and improve your time up to 2 minutes on a 40 km flat course.

Awareness of the importance of aerodynamics in improving time-trialling performance has seen the introduction of revolutionary materials and designs in cycling equipment. Wind tunnel studies have established accurately the amount of time that can be saved by using aerodynamic equipment and body positioning. This is summarised in Table 3.

It must be noted that the times mentioned are approximate as riding a stationary bicycle in a wind tunnel does not always resemble the different conditions which can be met on the road.

Table 3 shows the amount of time saved on a 40 km time trial through the use of aerodynamic components compared with conventional equipment and based on wind tunnel testing.

The figures cited are for a cyclist travelling at 36-38 kph. You save less time the faster you go since it takes you less time to ride a course at a faster speed.

Table 3

Aero handlebars .... approx. 2 min

Aero front wheel .... approx. 30-60 secs

Disc rear wheel .... approx. 20-40 secs

Aero frame .... approx. 20-40 secs

Aero helmet .... approx. 15-30 secs

A small additional aerodynamic advantage can be obtained by wearing a skinsuit; putting the drink bottle behind the seat; putting tape over shoe laces; mounting the pump under the top tube; shaving hair from arms and legs; removing the small chain ring; using an aerostem, crankset, brakeset and derailleurs; strapless pedals; thin, smooth, handlebar tape or none at all; and shift levers mounted side by side on top of the down tube (with the cable mounted inside the frame) rather than on the sides on the down tube. Tests so far have not shown an aerodynamic advantage in mounting the gearlevers onto the aerobars although it does add to convenience, especially on flat courses.

training aids

Rollers, windload and magnetically loaded trainers are not only useful training aids during a long winter but they can also be used during the season for specific strength and technique training.

Training on rollers enhances a smoother pedalling action and will teach you to ride in a straight line by improving balance. If you have not used rollers before, start between door posts for support because initially riding them will feel awkward.

Rollers can be used for easy workouts, e.g., 30 minutes spinning following a hard run, or for steady state riding for a longer period of time. This can be boring so a Walkman or television set can assist. The rollers can also be used for "speedplay" using bigger gears (52/53-15, 14, 13) and for repetitions maintaining a cadence between 80-100 rpm.

A hard 30-60 minute session on a windload or magnetically loaded trainer is a very efficient way of improving strength because of the extra resistance it provides. Resistance on windload trainers can be varied by changing gears. When using a magnetically loaded trainer, resistance can also be changed by changing the magnetic resistance. Increasing magnetic resistance simulates hill riding while the windload trainer is more like riding on a flat road.

Many indoor trainers now carry a combination of windloading and magnetically loading with precise computerised feedback on speed, load, time, distance and additional more or less relevant information.

This sophistication in indoor trainers has certainly made indoor workouts more interesting.

One hour on the windload trainer can be compared with two hours in the hills.

There are two basic workouts for the windload trainer.

The first one is that of shorter and longer repetitions. The standard example is a 5 min warm up followed by 5 x 4 mins repetitions with 1 minute easy in between. This is then followed by 5 mins steady and 10 mins of 1-legged exercises.

This is a technique which develops a smooth pedal stroke.

It is done by putting a leg on a chair next to the trainer and then riding with the other leg only, so as to avoid having one leg pushing down while the other leg is pulling up. Use a small gear and alternate legs after a few minutes or when one tires. After a few switches use both legs in a small gear and simulate your one-legged state by maintaining even pressure throughout the circle.

The session can be finished off with a steady 5 or 10 minute ride or some hard 2 minute repetitions with 2 minutes easy in between.

Many variations exist on this theme, variations in repetitions (the "ladder" is popular by which you do 2, 4, 6, 8, 6, 4, 2 minute repetitions with 1 or 2 minutes easy in between) and intensity. Lower intensities are used in the build up (general preparation phase) and higher intensities in the specific and competition phase.

A second workout is that of a controlled timetrial. Following a warm up do between 30-60 minutes of steady to hard, trying to maintain a certain speed or workload. Follow this with some easy cycling and/or one-legged exercises.

The intensity again depends on the stage of training and fitness.

It is fun to see improvement being made over a period of time, especially when you get accurate feedback from a computerised display.

12

running

Running is the most natural and basic movement of the three triathlon disciplines. Children run more, especially when they play, than they walk. Running is one of the most practical forms of exercise worldwide and is also the basic movement of many other sports. Indepth studies (whole conferences and symposiums) have been devoted to what makes us run. It is the simplest of all sports but has been studied the most with many publications available on the physiology, psychology and philosophy of running.

One of the more intriguing aspects of running is the "runner's high" which so far is poorly explained. Most triathletes will agree that there is no swimmer's or cyclist's high comparable with the euphoria of the runner's high - a state of emotional elation which does not come often but when present is extremely difficult to describe.

Despite it being simple in its execution, there are two factors which make the run the most demanding of the three disciplines.

1) It is the only discipline in which you have to carry your own body weight. In swimming and cycling we are supported by the water and the bike which protect us from the forces of gravity. The forces travelling up our legs caused by gravity when we are running are trebled compared with when we are walking. This means considerable strain on the bones, tendons, muscles and joints of the lower extremities with a subsequent increased risk of injury. Avoiding injury is always a main priority.

2) The run in a triathlon is not just a run. It is the last discipline and we start it in an already fatigued state. Some excellent runners who have ventured into triathlons with the idea of blitzing the field in the run have learned the hard way. The bike-to-run transition can upset you completely if you are not prepared.

The way in which you handle the fatigue accumulated from the two previous disciplines is the deciding factor in the final outcome of a race. Top contenders are usually aware of the importance of having something in reserve for the run even to the extent that they will wait for their pursuers to catch up in the bike section, confident that they can outrun them.

The great advantage of running is that you can do it almost anywhere. With swimming you are restricted to the availability of safe water and for biking, the requirement is for relatively smooth roads and reasonable weather conditions.

In running there are few terrain and weather restrictions, and dangers involved are minimal. It is also the least time consuming of the three disciplines, making it the most attractive, economical and fun way to gain fitness for the working person.

running technique

Bill Bowerman, a well known running coach, defined running as follows :

A running stride is a complete cycle of weight-bearing or support on one foot followed by a period of non weight-bearing or "float" then a period of weight-bearing on the other foot and another period of "float".

Different sports require different styles of running and we will concentrate mainly on the styles for a middle distance /long distance runner, applicable to both short and long distance triathlons.

posture

Running efficiency and style are very much related to posture. The most efficient running position is erect (straight back) which is achieved by a backward tilt of the pelvis. If the pelvis is pushed forward it results in a sway back position which allows limited hip movement and a shift of the centre of gravity too far forward. For the middle distance runner (and short distance triathlete) a slight forward lean is allowed (up to 10 degrees) as this will contribute to speed.

A straight posture will help the neck and shoulder muscles relax. It is important that the upper body is relaxed so you feel comfortable, can breathe freely and your arm action can contribute to the running movement.

stride length

Research has not come up with a uniform formula for an optimal stride length as yet. Studies show that the most efficient stride length is the one that the runner feels most comfortable with and so differs for every athlete. It is the foot plant which decides the stride length. The more efficient runners intuitively land their foot under the body's centre of gravity (navel) and under their slightly flexed knee. The leg should never be fully extended in front of the body.

A relatively short stride is most efficient which means that it is better to understride than overstride. This is especially so for the marathon section of a long distance triathlon. A short stride with faster leg turnover combined with a low knee position and a low back kick will result in an efficient shuffle which can be kept up for long periods. For shorter distances speed can be increased by increasing stride length and knee lift, resulting in a slightly lower leg turnover and a higher back kick.

One of the most common errors is overstriding. This brakes the forward motion by planting the foot in front of the centre of gravity. Overstriding will also result in an exaggerated bounce, further increasing the workload.

foot plant

A proper foot plant will occur almost naturally by keeping the knees slightly bent at all times and by not overstriding. A properly executed foot plant can greatly contribute to running style and plays a major role in prevention of injury.

The foot plant is underneath the centre of gravity, the knee is slightly bent and first contact with the ground is made with the outer edge of the heel.

One way to find out about your own foot plant is to check the wear pattern on the sole of a pair of older running shoes. They should be worn down more at the outside of the heel (landing) and under the ball of the foot towards the big toe (push-off).

The foot plant is underneath the centre of gravity, the knee is slightly bent and first contact with the ground is made with the outer edge of the heel. The foot then rolls forward and inward. The inward motion (pronation) has a shock-absorbing effect. The push-off comes from the ball of the foot and the big toe.

Sprinters usually contact the ground first on the outside edge high on the ball of the foot.

The contact point lies further back towards the heel as the distance being attempted increases with a heel landing at any distance over 1500 metres.

"Toe running" is one of the recognised causes of common injuries such as shin splints, plantar fasciitis and as a contributor to stress fractures. A cross-over foot plant whereby the foot lands across the body's midline results in over pronation and can subsequently cause injury.

arm action
The hands and arms, when used properly, can add to drive and balance. The arms swing in rhythm with the legs in a relaxed way, swinging slightly across the chest. The fingers need to be slightly clenched with the thumb on the index finger. The wrist is firm in line with the forearms with the elbow bent to approximately 90 degrees. A proper arm swing will result in relaxation and minimal movement of the shoulder and neck muscles.

breathing
Breathing should be done in a rhythmic fashion in time with the foot plant. The rhythm depends on running speed. For easy running inhale every four steps, then exhale after four, increasing the ratio 3:3 or even 2:2 when the pace picks up. Concentrating on breathing in a rhythmic fashion or counting 1, 2, 3 (inhale), 1, 2, 3 (exhale) is a good meditation device and can take your mind off fatigue, pain and/or adverse weather conditions.

Inhale through your mouth, exhale through your nose and mouth. Include the diaphragm (the muscular partition between chest and abdomen) in your breathing pattern by taking deep breaths. This prevents superficial breathing and the much-dreaded side stitch.

Diaphragmic breathing can be checked by putting your hand on your upper abdomen when running. You should feel an up (breathing in) and down (breathing out) movement of your abdomen.

hill running
Hill running is as much psychological as it is physical. Uphill running, especially when done as a time trial or repetitions, is an excellent way of increasing endurance, strength, speed and tolerance of fatigue. It should be part of any serious triathlete's training armoury.

Training on the flat will not prepare you for hill racing, but hill training will not only prepare you for hill racing, it will also improve your running ability on the flat. The technique of running uphill differs from running on the flat in that there is much more forward lean (lean into the hill).

On steep hills stay on the balls of your feet but on more gentle inclines stick to a heel landing. The knees need to be lifted a bit higher and the arms are used more than on the flat. The psychology of hill running is not to be afraid and not to look up.

When running downhill the impact on each foot strike is dramatically increased with subsequent exposure to injury. Therefore, any downhill running done in training should be easy and executed with control. When running downhill in a race try and overcome your natural instinct to lean back and put on the brakes. Let gravity do the work. Lean forward, keep the upper body perpendicular to the ground, lengthen your stride but otherwise run with the same action and foot plant as on the flat.

shoes

One of the worst things human beings have done in the process of evolution is to put on shoes. This has undermined the natural function of the foot, which is to support our body when standing or moving, to such an extent that we are now fully dependent on footwear. The continuous artificial and static support from footwear has eroded and weakened the natural and more functional support mechanism of the foot, which has resulted in a tremendous increase in ailments affecting our locomotive system from the foot up to the neck.

There are studies which show that barefoot runners are almost immune to injury as a consequence of the superior functioning of a well-conditioned, unsupported foot. For most of us, it is too late to go back to nature and we will have to accept that our cupboards will contain a certain number of used and new shoes assembled in the search for right footwear. As there is no superior model or design, and as every foot is different, choosing the right running shoes is a personal matter.

Running shoes come in three different shapes: straight, slightly curved, and curved. The straighter the shoe the more support it gives but a curved shoe gives better mobility to the foot.

There are also three different types of construction:

1) board-lasting - a fibreboard runs from the heel to the fore foot;
2) slip-lasting - no board, just stitching;
3) combination-lasting - a board that runs from the heel to mid-foot with stitching the rest of the way.

Board-lasted shoes have greater stability, slip-lasted shoes provide more comfort and flexibility and combination-lasting provides stability for the rear of the foot and comfort for the forefoot. The materials the mid-sole and outer sole are made of are continually being upgraded. Mid-soles are currently made of a combination of EVA (ethylene vinyl actate) and polyurethane. EVA provides the cushioning and polyurethane is added for reinforcement. The outer sole is made of rubber compounds. The harder the compound the greater its durability but also its weight. The heel counter (the cup built into the rear of the shoe) is made of durable plastic and assists in controlling excessive foot motion.

In the last decade most running shoe designers have concentrated on improving foot cushioning and support.

Recently Adidas has recognised that, rather than propping up our feet more and more, perhaps we should go back to a shoe which allows for as much natural movement of the foot as possible.

Assisted by independent research, they found that the small movement in the midfoot around the horizontal axis, called torsion, is essential for running and walking and has been overlooked by shoe manufacturers so far.

Adidas came up with the torsion bar, built into the sole of the shoe, which allows the foot to move more naturally, thereby mimicking barefoot running more closely.

Already early studies show a reduction of injuries in runners who wear this type of shoe.

Further research and time will tell if this basically simple idea is as revolutionary as it is said to be.

The three important factors to consider when buying a pair of running shoes are:

1. Running style: foot plant is an important factor in our running style. There are roughly three types of foot plants:

    (a) the pronator, whereby the ankle deviates inwards on foot plant;
    (b) the neutral foot, whereby the ankle is straight on foot plant, and
    (c) the supinator, whereby the ankle deviates outwards on foot plant.

    Most of us are pronators or neutral runners, requiring an anti-pronation shoe (which is firmer on the inside of the shoe sole) or a neutral shoe. Orthotics might be required for runners with excessive rear foot motion or other foot problems.

2. Weight: heavier runners in general need more support.

3. Running surface: soft surfaces require a firmer shoe and if you run on harder surfaces, choose a more cushioned shoe.

If you have normal feet you can usually choose from a variety of different shoes, focusing on comfort. A flat-footed runner is best suited to a straight, board-lasted shoe with plenty of rear support. Flat feet tend to pronate too much and might require some form of arch support if injuries to the lower extremities occur frequently. A high-arched (rigid) foot wants as much mobility as it can get and is suited to a slip-lasted shoe.

When buying shoes be aware of your foot type. Specialist shops for runners and other sportspersons often have staff with a background in running and who have been trained in assessing the customer's needs. Sports-medicine physicians, sports physiotherapists and podiatrists are also able to give you general advice on what type of shoes will suit your feet. But, within that advice, picking the right shoes still remains your responsibility.

- Never buy shoes when you are in a hurry. Take your time.
- Be prepared to try different designs and models to get a feel for what is comfortable and what is not. For example, try board-lasted shoes and compare with slip-lasted or combination-lasted shoes.
- If store policy permits, take a short walk or jog in each pair.
- Do not assume that sizing is universal. Sizes differ according to models.
- There should be approximately the width of a thumb nail between the end of your longest (not always your biggest) toe and the end of the shoe. If the shoes are too small you will end up with blisters and black nails. To compensate for foot-swelling when running, it is safer to go for a slightly larger shoe.
- The heel should fit snugly into the back of the shoe with no up and down movement.
- Make sure that the shoes have proper cushioning under the heels for shock absorption. (Racing flats compromise in this area as they have to be light.)
- A stiff mid-sole of the shoe can contribute to achilles tendon problems and plantar fasciitis.
- If you have abnormally wide or narrow feet select a model which comes in different width sizes.
- Replace shoes frequently, especially if you are prone to injury. Once shoes require repairs they have usually lost their spring and support. Patching up and resoling old shoes is best avoided if finance allows.
- Do not compromise fit and comfort for cost. The crucial factor in selecting shoes is always the fit and comfort.
- Break the shoes in slowly by alternating them with your old pairs.
- If you have found a model which suits you and keeps you injury free, stick to it.

Racing flats have less stability and cushioning than training shoes and should only be used when racing by the more competitive triathlete. The advantage of racing flats is their lightness, which helps you to run slightly faster and gives you a psychological lift, something you can do with as you enter the third stage of the race.

Racing shoes are not for everyone, however. Heavy runners (more than 80 kg) may generate too much force through the legs to be safe in them and injury may result.

In longer races, like a marathon, the advantage of lightness might be outweighed by the cumulative effect of the pounding. This is especially so when hard surfaces such as concrete are encountered.

13 stretching

Many athletes, coaches and sports medicine experts consider stretching exercises to be an important part of conditioning for sports.

In the triathlon stretching plays a role especially in injury prevention and treatment, thereby indirectly contributing to performance. Flexibility is only a minor component of fitness for swimming, biking and running and, therefore, more flexible triathletes do not necessarily have a performance advantage.

However, there is some indication that an increased stiffness in muscle groups can contribute to overuse injury. For example, there is a direct relationship between stiffness of the shoulder and the risk of developing swimmer's shoulder.

In general, strengthening of muscles will always be combined with a slight shortening of the affected muscle group. Together with a reduction in elasticity which comes with ageing, increased strength can contribute to inflexibility. This can be counteracted by appropriate flexibility programmes.

Many studies on stretching conclude that stretching does not contribute to injury prevention and in some cases can even increase the risk of injury. The reason for that finding is most likely the fact that many athletes do not stretch properly. It is extremely important to use proper stretching techniques as otherwise harm can be done.

The technique of stretching discussed in this chapter is the contract-relax-stretch technique. There is evidence that contracting the muscle prior to the stretch gives a more effective lengthening. This is achieved by an isometric (muscle length stays static) contraction of the muscle group concerned for 6-10 seconds against an immovable resistance.

stretching techniques

Following are some of the basic rules related to this technique of stretching.

- Stretching is best done following a light warm up and/or at the conclusion of a training session. Cold muscles do not stretch well and, therefore, the commonly used routine of stretching before a workout is far less effective.
- Contract the concerned muscle group for 6-10 seconds, then relax for 2-3 seconds before stretching for 10-20 seconds.
- Repeat each contract relax stretch cycle 2-3 times.
- Stretch slowly and gradually. Do not bounce.
- Breathe in a relaxed way during the contract and stretch phases. Do not hold your breath.
- Regularity is the most Important factor in stretching. A daily programme will offer the best results.
- Do not compare yourself with others when stretching. Always stay within your own limits.
- Stretching should never hurt.

recommended stretches

Following are some examples of commonly used stretches for the major muscle groups related to swimming, cycling and running.

stretch 1

muscles:
back of shoulder (deltoids)
discipline:
swimming
contract:
lift elbow in front of cheek and push forwards and out with force.

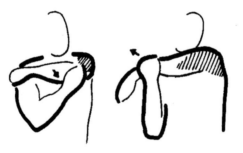

stretch:
push the elbow towards the opposite shoulder till you feel a good stretch at the back of the shoulder.

stretch 2

muscles:
back of upper arm and upper side of back (triceps, deltoids, latissimus and teres minor)
discipline:
swimming
contract:
lift elbow up beside head and push against resistance, e.g. a wall, or hold with the other hand.

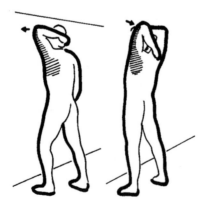

stretch:
pull the elbow back and down using the other hand.

stretch 3

muscles:
back of thighs (hamstrings)
discipline:
running
contract:
stand with leg straight
resting on low stool with
knee straight. Other support
leg should be slightly bent
with foot pointing straight
forward. Push heel against
the stool as hard as
possible.

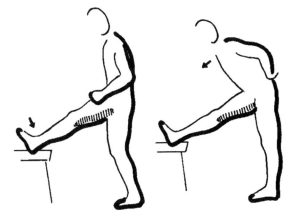

stretch:
bend forward in the hip with
straight back. Reach
forward with hands towards
toes or keep hands on back
to make sure back stays
straight. An alternative way
of stretching is to keep
upright and rotate the upper
body towards the extended
leg till you feel a stretch.

stretch 4

muscles:
calves (gastrocnemius)
discipline:
running
contract:
lean against wall. Place one
leg back with straight knee,
foot pointing forward. Bend
front leg slightly. Push toes
of rear foot hard into the
floor.

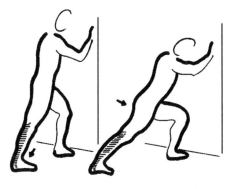

stretch:
push forward while holding
pelvis and hip straight.

stretch 5:

muscles:
calf (soleus) and achilles
tendon
discipline:
running
contract:
lean against wall. Place one
leg slightly back and bend
knee. Push toes of rear foot
hard into the floor.

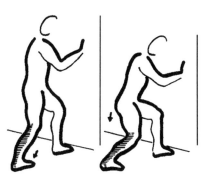

stretch:
bend the knee of the back
leg further while lowering
the hip.

Stretch 6

Muscles:
front of thigh (quadriceps)
and hip (iliopsoas)
Discipline:
running and cycling
Contract:
stand back with one leg
supporting upper body on
other bent leg with hands.
Push the back leg
downwards.

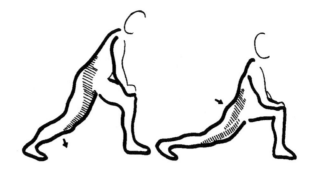

Stretch:
push the hip of the back leg
forwards. Keep the pelvis
and back straight. A
variation is to put the back
knee on the ground before
pushing the pelvis and hip
forward.

Stretch 7

Muscles:
insides of thighs (adductors)
Discipline:
cycling and running
Contract:
sit on floor with knees bent.
Place forearm between legs
and push hard inwards.

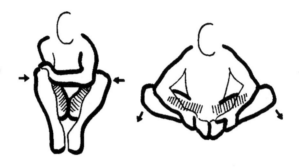

Stretch:
grab ankles with hands and
push knees down and out.

Stretch 8

Muscles:
outside of thigh (ilio-tibial
band) and buttock (gluteus
group)
Discipline:
running and cycling
Contract:
lean sideways against wall.
Keep supporting arm
straight. Put the inside leg
behind the front leg in
extended position while
bending the front leg
slightly. Push the outside of
the rear foot against the
floor.

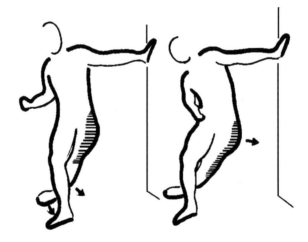

Stretch:
push the outside hip in with
the outside hand bending
the hip towards the wall,
"sinking" into the stretch
position.

14

racing

factors affecting performance

Racing performance is not only decided by proper physical preparation. Mental attitude (e.g. realistic goal setting) and nutritional strategies are as important for the competitive triathlete. Other factors like equipment, terrain and climatic conditions can all play a role. Most of those factors we can control to some extent. The factors affecting performance that we cannot control are our age, sex and genetic constitution which includes our body build and talent.

Talent is probably the single most deciding factor relating to racing performance. In general, a less talented athlete needs to do everything right to be able to beat a more talented athlete on the day and this will still depend on the talented athlete having a bad day.

However, in the triathlon many factors decide the outcome of a race besides talent. For example, triathletes can have a different level of talent for swimming, cycling and running. This makes the outcome of races less predictable. Many moderately talented athletes perform well through sheer commitment, discipline and proper application of training principles. Many highly talented triathletes come and go as they cannot find the dedication which is required to excel in this sport. Fig. 1 summarises all factors affecting triathlon performance. Of those factors only the endogenous factors are outside our control. The challenge is to get the best out of the remaining factors when aiming for optimum performance.

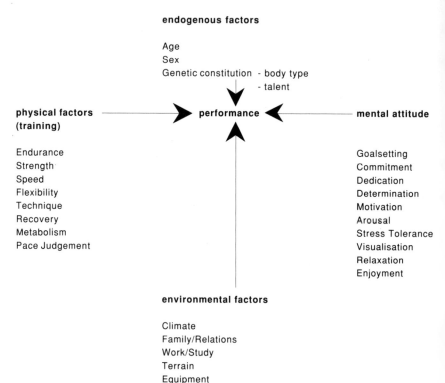

endogenous factors

Age
Sex
Genetic constitution - body type
                      - talent

physical factors ———————→ performance ←——————— mental attitude
(training)

Endurance   Goalsetting
Strength   Commitment
Speed   Dedication
Flexibility   Determination
Technique   Motivation
Recovery   Arousal
Metabolism   Stress Tolerance
Pace Judgement   Visualisation
                                                            Relaxation
                                                            Enjoyment

environmental factors

Climate
Family/Relations
Work/Study
Terrain
Equipment
Nutrition

Fig. 1.

Factors affecting
performance

The endogenous factors we can only accept. That is the base we have to work
from.

The physical factors we can work on by applying proper training principles as
discussed in the relevant chapters. This also includes training with a purpose and
training according to a plan without being inflexible. This means that you need to
be prepared to take other factors (weather, other commitments, illness etc.) into
consideration. That can mean missing, changing or swapping sessions, for
example using the wind load trainer rather than going outside.

It is unusual for a triathlete's preparation to go completely smoothly. Learning to
accept this rather than fight it or give up, will enhance your final performance.

One of the more significant mental factors affecting race outcome is realistic goal
setting. Too many athletes set themselves high goals for every race they do. More
often than not they end up disappointed. Many (especially males) overestimate
their ability, some (more common among women) underestimate their talents.
Especially for long distance events, first timers should only aim to finish in a
reasonable condition. From the experience gained more specific goal setting can
be done for the next race.

In general, it is better to set goals a little lower, rather than too high, as they are
more easily achieved, thereby preventing continuing disappointments. Set high

goals only for "do or die" races e.g., championships or selection races, but only when relatively experienced.

The most important physical factor during an endurance race is pace judgement. This can only be learnt by applying proper training methods and being in tune with your body and mind when training and racing. Heart rate monitors can assist in pace judgement but should never overrule the body/mind language.

race strategies

Plan your race well in advance, know your strengths and work around these.

pre-race stage 1
You will have trained towards a specific race for weeks or perhaps months. You have done the work, time trials and have completed at least the distances required in each specific race. If a 90 km cycle is involved you should have done this distance at least three times in your training so be confident in your abilities, but know your limitations and do not plan to take many minutes off each leg.

pre-race stage 2
When the day prior to the race arrives, you will have seen over the course, possibly even trained over it many times. You should now be resting. Never be "psyched out" by any course as each race holds a little in store for everyone.

This is the time to put one or two hours' mental thought into the race. Realise your strengths and plan accordingly. Never think you are not good at one of the three disciplines, but rather, that this is the leg you must work on. If you are a poor swimmer, plan to complete your swim as best you can and feel good about finishing it and getting into your stronger disciplines. If you are a strong cyclist, plan to work hard on this section and proceed as far up the field as you can. Feel good about passing people but do not think the cycle leg is the total race - there is still the run to come. Depending on how you run, plan to maintain, pass or even be passed. Be positive about this and always remember the triathlon has specialists in each discipline. The person who is passing you now, you may pass later.

pre-race stage 3
The morning of the race. Relax and have a few minutes by yourself. Go over the course in your mind and reiterate your thoughts of the previous day. Look forward to the event and be determined to enjoy it (some of us have a weird sense of enjoyment).

race strategy
Your race strategy is to stick to your race plan. However, there is nothing wrong with having more than one race plan, allowing for flexibility during the race. Do not change your plan one minute before the race because someone you know, or maybe even train with, is doing something different. Remember you know your abilities best.

Now is not the time to change your race plan.

race day

By race day all the hard work has been done. In fact, you have probably completed the hardest and most challenging part, the preparation itself.

You need to be highly organised for race day so that on the morning of the event you are not flustered in any way. To achieve this, on the day prior to the race, complete all the physical tasks associated with your participation, such as preparing your bike, pinning race numbers on tops and checking your wetsuit, shoes and bike shoes. All the clothing and equipment you will require in the race should be ready the day before - a day when most athletes have a rest day. This is also a constructive way of battling nerves by giving you something to do and will mean that on race day it should be only a matter of getting up and travelling to the race start.

You need to rise at least two hours before the race (many athletes require more time) so you can have a light breakfast, after which you need 15 minutes completely to yourself prior to setting off to the race start.

This 15 minutes is a time of great importance, a time when you are alone. This is when you visualise what is ahead. You will have been over the course prior to the event and will know what to expect. During this time relax and try to visualise the entire race from start to finish. Work out where you want to be in the water, the start itself, your position and thoughts 400 m into the swim after the mad helter-skelter at the start, the settling into a good stroke rate while concentrating on technique. As the swim comes to an end think about what is going to happen as you get out of the water - your transition, how your clothes and equipment are set up, where your bike is amongst the possible 1200 other cycles, getting on the bike and getting into a solid strong pace and not labouring too hard on gears. Visualise how you will feel in the race itself remembering perhaps some of the important gear changes, the steeper hills or the cornering on the bike. Then comes another transition into the run. Think of the ways you will relax if you are feeling tight - perhaps drop the shoulders slightly to feel easier. Concentrate on some small fault such as starting the race too fast and dying in the latter stages.

Be sure you know where your bike is.

You need the 15 minutes to think of all these factors and to calm yourself. To prevent becoming uptight, formulate what you are going to do or how you are going to race. This has all been planned days and weeks before and is now completely reviewed one more time during this precious and most important visualisation period.

There may be a few things that have to be changed on race day and this is where flexibility acquired during training comes in. You may need to change clothing because of the weather or have other small adjustments to make. By rising early you have time to make these alterations.

The next step is getting to the race start. This is an extremely tense place, an area where you really need to think entirely of yourself and your own race, and not get carried away with what is happening around you. The tension and hype just prior to the start can be draining to an athlete and can be quite daunting. Many athletes have their own routines which they indulge in to get them through this demanding period. Many triathletes now use headphones to listen to their favourite music.

How you tackle this period is often dictated by your aspirations for the race. If you want only to finish the race, this period can be exciting but it is still a time you need for yourself to do your own thing.

Do not be daunted by the bikes that everyone else has and you do not; the cycling shoes you do not possess or the funny wheels or aerodynamic handlebars that may be on other cycles. Do not forget to turn your running shoes upside down when it rains.

Many triathletes listen to their favourite music while focusing on the race ahead.

You are at the start, you have hours and weeks of solid training behind you and now is not the time to start comparing your equipment with that of everyone else.

checkpoints
There are a few major checkpoints that have to be attended to on race day.

* You probably will have taken your bike to the cycle start by car so check your gears and see that your wheels are on properly. If you have left your bike at the start overnight, which is becoming a common practice, again check the tyres and the brakes. Go for a short ride and get your bike in the right gear - a factor that is commonly overlooked. You want to start off in the appropriate gear. If you are going straight up a hill you need to be in an easy gear.
* You need to keep warm prior to the start so there is no need to be changed 40 minutes beforehand. Ensure that you are always warm. Obviously, on cold days this is particularly important.
* Keep hydrated, especially if it is a hot day. Many athletes walk around with a bidon of water or diluted fruit juice. You can still be drinking up to 15 minutes before the race.
* Get into the right frame of mind before the start. Stop panicking. Everything is done now so sit and feel good about it. A positive attitude about the race is half the battle.
* Pay attention to your warm up and optional stretching exercises. Unlike

training, where you can gradually increase your tempo as your body warms and your muscles stretch, the madcap fury of the first few hundred metres of the swim require your muscles, joints and tendons to be relaxed and warm.

the swim

At the swim start you should always seed yourself according to your own ability. It does not help you or anyone else if a slow swimmer is at the front. You will get swum over, goggles will be knocked off and psychologically you will feel battered with everyone passing.

At the start of the swim, seed yourself to avoid being "swum over" by faster swimmers.

Try to find landmarks in the swim. It is not always possible, especially in heavy seas where both landmarks and marker buoys can be obscured. If you have included this discipline in your training schedule it will make it so much easier on race day. During training you will have taught yourself to swim in a straight line in open water and the straighter you swim from buoy to buoy the less strokes you require to finish the course; the time will be faster and you will have more energy when tackling the cycling and running that lie ahead. You will have gained your first advantage in the race.

The first 200-400 m of the swim will often be the fastest. Competitors race away from the start in a combination of the release of pent-up energies, and the need to break away from the main bunch in order to settle into a good, steady, unencumbered stroke.

Some sprint training carried out in the build up will have acclimatised your body to this explosive beginning and this allows you to settle quickly into a good steady rhythm. It often means getting out with a much faster pack at the start of the swim and they will drag you through to a quicker time. This is extremely important to the elite triathletes. If they get on to the wrong set of toes during the swim it can mean the difference of several placings heading into the cycle leg.

Make sure you wear a swim cap. It not only helps prevent cold by curbing heat loss but gives a streamline effect - the same as Olympic swimmers attain by shaving their heads. A wetsuit is of great advantage also. It is legal and as long as it is well fitting with a smooth surface for streamlining, it will keep your body far more buoyant, putting you in a better position in the water. This will enable you to achieve a much faster swim time. For lesser swimmers a wetsuit is worth up to three minutes in a 1500 metre event.

Once into your settled pace in the swim get your rhythm going and control your breathing. Quite often, for the lesser swimmers, it is a trying time but do not panic. You know you can cover the distance. Keep your cool and concentrate on maintaining that steady breathing pattern. Towards the end of the leg start focusing your attention on the transition.

the first transition
There are many products available now to make for a faster transition - clip pedals and special toggles on your shoelaces, for example.

Slow swimmers are often confronted with chaos in the transition.

Many of the elite triathletes will have their shoes attached to their bike pedals and will have practised mounting their bike, cycling along the road and then getting their feet into their bike shoes.

As helmets are now compulsory in all triathlons, you should ensure that you have some form of quick fastening device.

For comfort, and if you are only looking to finish the race, it is fine to have a bucket of water to wash your feet to get rid of unwanted sand, a towel to dry yourself down, a pair of socks or an extra jersey if it is cold. This all takes time but it is perfectly all right if you are aiming only to finish. But, if you are there to race or better a previous time, then all these factors can mean an extra two minutes on your total time - an equivalent of about 500 metres at the end of the running leg which is quite significant.

the bike
Once on the bike you need to get quickly into a settled rhythm. Before starting out, fasten helmets.Once on the bike tighten shoes, perhaps have a drink to get the salty taste out of your mouth and to hydrate yourself again. This should not take long as you will want to get into your rhythm as quickly as possible.

You do not want to take off on the bike, get into a hyperventilating pace and become as tense as a board. You need to relax and get into a good strong pace where you will find the going much easier than if you take off at a fast, unrealistic pace and are tense with it. This is where your pacing comes in because you will slip naturally into your own rhythm. Do not try to keep up with anyone near you, just do your own thing.

Cycle as close to the centre of the road as safety permits, for two main reasons. Any broken glass tends to accumulate at the side and also the camber of the road is such that when biking there you feel as though you are on the edge, you seem to be pedalling uphill all the time.

Do not fall into lazy habits concerning gear changes and attempt to climb a hill, for instance, in a gear that is not best suited to the gradient just to save the effort of actually changing from one gear to another. You will find usually that before you get halfway up the hill you will begin to stall and the going will get far tougher than if you had selected the correct gear earlier.

It is absolutely important, when cycling, to remember to drink. Sometimes athletes can get so involved with their cycling and so carried away by the whole event, that they forget to take their liquids. Be hydrated at all times - the amount of fluid needed will depend on the distance of the event and the temperature. Your training will tell you how much you need.

Currently the biggest threat to the enjoyment of the triathlon is the drafting debate in relation to the cycling leg. Although the I.T.U. has set clear rules, many countries use variations on those rules. Even different races in the same country can have a different set of rules.

Then there is the problem of policing the rules. There are as yet very few properly trained and experienced draftbusters. As a consequence many disqualifications are successfully appealed, but also whole bunches are disqualified by overzealous draftbusters.

The more competitive the triathlon becomes, the more the sport grows, the uglier the debate will become.

For a competitive triathlete it is extremely frustrating and against all their instincts to "fall back" when being passed. The intuitive response is to get back in front and so the appearance of a "rolling bunch" is created.

The whole drafting rule needs to be reassessed. Already the penalty has been changed from instant disqualification to a stop and restart policy which makes sense. However, other solutions need to be considered. Perhaps drafting needs to be made legal as it is for swimming and running. It would certainly change the sport, but not necessarily for the worse. It could give it another exciting dimension.

the second transition
As the cycling leg nears completion thoughts will turn to the final leg, the run. For the last 400-600 m of the bike leg change into an easy gear so that you are pedalling at a higher cadence. Doing this will help remove the lactic acid build-up in your muscles. Perhaps have your last good drink. Often there is not an aid station at the beginning of the run so you need to build up your fluids before commencing the final leg.

Your shoes will be ready and prepared with either velcro, elastic laces, or toggle fasteners to give you a quick transition. You may also have a small drink bottle which you wish to carry in the race. There will be an elastic strip with your number on it or a numbered tee-shirt to put on. The athlete who only wants to finish sometimes has a complete change at this stage but for the person seeking a time or a placing, the least number of clothes that have to be changed the better.

This transition should not take long. If you have your feet out of your bike shoes, then all you need do is put your cycle on its rack, your feet into your waiting running shoes, number on and away. And do not forget to take your helmet off.

the run
Again, the same criteria apply at the start of the running leg as before. Immediately get into a pace which is applicable to you. Remember that it will take approximately a kilometre to lose that awkward feeling of rubbery legs and poor control. After that your running will fall into place automatically. Even during a 10 km leg there is no need to race madly from the moment you dismount from your bike. Once you are at the halfway or turnaround point then it is time to increase your tempo. Start looking at competitors ahead and gradually try and overtake them. It is when you are within about 4 km of the finish that an all out effort should be made.

Remember to keep drinking at all times. Even in cool conditions it is possible to dehydrate. But, never try a drink which you have not taken in training.

short triathlons

Comfort is not so important but is still a major factor in short triathlons. We can get away with things such as competing in togs, but footwear is still of utmost importance.

Do not take short cuts that you are not used to and that have not been tried during training (e.g., no socks in a race may lead to blisters which will cost you minutes as opposed to seconds if you had put on socks).

long triathlons

Comfort, temperature control and nutrition are of prime importance in a long triathlon. Take time to organise all of these well. This normally means changing after each discipline and drying off to avoid chafing. Wear extras such as gloves, cycle shorts, a hat during the race and sunglasses, things that you may not need for short events. Take time to drink and eat, especially during the bike and the run. Do not stop unnecessarily, however, as it is hard to start again.

equipment for racing

pre-race

- Warm clothing
- Water bottle for pre-race hydration, containing water and/or carbohydrate replacement fluid
- Toilet paper

swim

- Togs
- Singlet
- Race number on singlet or elastic band
- Wetsuit
- Caps (2 if cold)
- Goggles
- Vaseline (to prevent chafing)
- Towel (for drying or standing on during transition).

cycle

- Bike (you will not be the first person to forget it)
- Drink bidons (filled)
- Food (for long distance events)
- Pump, including pressure gauge
- Hardshell helmet
- Cycling shoes
- Spare tubular tyre, prestretched, and tyre levers (if using clinchers)
- Gloves if required
- Cycle top if required for longer races; cycle shorts.
- Computer, if required
- Race number
- Safety pins (somebody is always looking for them)
- Socks if required

run

- Shoes
- Running top and shorts if required
- Sunhat if required
- Vaseline if required
- Small water bottle

Have a happy and enjoyable race. Remember, the only person you have to prove anything to is yourself!

Matt Brick, world duathlon champion, carefully monitors his training and performance levels to guard against overtraining.

15

nutrition

Ien Hellemans (B. Dietetics, Groningen, Postgrad. Dip. Sc., Otago; Certificate in Sports Nutrition, Canberra) combines her specialist knowledge as a nutritionist with that of an athlete. A competitive swimmer in her native country, the Netherlands (she also successfully completed the world famous 1992 Coast-to-Coast multi-endurance event as part of a two person team) she was drawn into the field of sports nutrition, especially nutrition relating to endurance sports such as triathlons, firstly via the performances of her husband, John, and then through guiding Erin Baker. She has her own nutrition consultancy where she advises individual athletes and is a consultant to several New Zealand sporting associations.

The majority of triathletes are well aware of the importance of nutrition in achieving maximum results in both training and racing. The best dietary strategies will support intense training programmes, contribute to the best possible race results and to optimal health, a crucial asset for any athlete. Research during the '80s has greatly enhanced our knowledge on the specific dietary needs of triathletes and although several issues remain unresolved, it is now possible to provide detailed guidelines for training, competition, recovery and the prevention or management of particular problems.

Triathletes have unique dietary needs dictated by training frequency, volume and intensity as well as gender, age, body size and health status. Specific requirements may change over time depending on training years, training phase, racing distance (short versus long course triathlon) and the possible presence of nutritional deficiencies.

In achieving optimum nutrition you may, however, come across some obstacles. It is not easy to be a triathlete. Unless you are a pro you very likely have to balance training with work or study commitments and perhaps family responsibilities. You may live in a flat, having to fend for yourself or being dependent on the food that others prepare which may or may not be suitable. Your budget may be tight and not stretch far enough to accommodate your need for large amounts of food and possibly supplements. Finally, like most people in Western countries, your taste buds may have adjusted to, and prefer, the high fat foods we tend to eat in our part of the world. The last thing a triathlete needs is a high fat diet. Although these problems may seem insurmountable initially, you will find that by first knowing what your requirements are and then planning for them, things will fall into place fairly quickly. Remember that goal setting, planning ahead and keeping things simple and practical are the key ingredients to implementing a successful nutritional programme.

nutritional needs of triathletes

There are several basic strategies underpinning the more specific requirements induced by triathlon training. They can be summarised as follows:

1. **Choose a wide variety of foods.** Eating a selection of foods every day guarantees an adequate intake of all essential nutrients. The Four Food Groups provide your framework for variety.

   four food groups

   Breads and cereal foods
   Fruits and vegetables
   Milk and milk products
   Meat, fish, chicken, eggs, pulses,
   nuts, seeds or soy foods.

2. **Eat plenty of carbohydrate foods.** Secure a high intake of nutritious carbohydrates such as wholegrain breads and cereals, rice, pasta, pulses (e.g. lentils, kidney beans, baked beans), potatoes, vegetables and fruits.

3. **Limit intake of fats.** High fat consumption does not contribute to optimum health or performance. Go easy on foods like butter, margarine, oils, mayonnaise, cream, sour cream, cream cheese and limit consumption of cakes, pastries, pies, chocolate, crisps and fried or takeaway food. Some foods, although high in fat, do contain significant amounts of essential nutrients and should be used wisely. This group includes cheeses, icecream, nuts/seeds, peanut butter and tahini.

4. **Drink plenty of fluids.** An adequate fluid consumption is crucial. The average person requires 2.5 litres of fluid per day and triathletes need this plus a lot more to compensate for large fluid losses during training. It is essential to drink plenty of water every day.

5. **Go easy on salt.** Salt consumption is very high in the typical Western diet. It is likely that many triathletes consume too much and although a small amount is needed it is best to limit salt used in cooking and at the table and to be careful with high salt foods.

6. **Be cautious with alcohol.** Although it is unnecessary to eliminate alcohol,

consumption should be incidental and moderate. Alcohol lowers blood glucose levels, acts as a diuretic and affects the central nervous system, all of which have a detrimental effect on performance. If you want to drink, do so in moderation (avoid binges) and avoid alcohol altogether on the days before competition, immediately after competition and in the build up to your major events.

Fig.1 summarises the above guidelines.

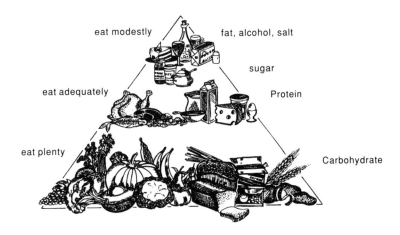

Fig. 1.

The triathlete's food pyramid (adapted from the Australian Nutrition Foundation).

training diet

Now that basic principles have been outlined you are ready to have a closer look at your specific needs. These will be determined by the type of programme you follow (e.g. cyclic training), mileage, intensity and frequency of training and number of sessions per day. Physical activity outside training influences dietary requirements also and your lifestyle will affect the amount of time and energy you have to plan, purchase and prepare food/meals. The sum total of these factors will determine your day-to-day eating patterns.

energy

The major dietary need is for a significantly increased energy (kilojoule or kilocalorie) intake. Those who train for middle or long course and competitive short course triathletes have the highest energy needs. Males have higher requirements compared with females (because of a larger lean body mass) and adolescents have increased requirements to compensate for physical growth. There are two levels of energy expenditure to consider. Firstly, a certain amount of energy is required to maintain normal body functions and daily activity while additional energy is needed to support training. **Tables 1 and 2** provide estimated energy needs for both categories. Let's consider Judy, a competitive short course triathlete. She is 25 years old and weighs 60 kg. Her estimated daily energy requirement is 9200 kJoules or 2190 kCalories **(see Table 1)**. On Mondays she swims for 60 minutes in the morning and cycles for 90 minutes in the afternoon. Using Table 2 we can estimate that she will expend 2340 kJoules during her swim and 3690 on her cycle ride (assuming she bikes at 25 km/hr). Total energy requirement for that Monday is, therefore, 9200 plus 6030 equals 15230 kJoules (3626 kCalories). Keep in mind that this is an estimate only; the calculation does not account for individual variability. As daily training programmes vary so will daily energy needs fluctuate. It is important to balance kJoule intake from food with energy expenditure through training. Failing to regularly consume adequate energy will result in fatigue, loss of lean body weight and a decrease in performance while overconsumption will lead to weight gain or more precisely, fat gain. Both are of course undesirable.

Table 1   **estimated daily energy requirements**

		energy requirement (in kJoules[1])	
	body weight (in kg)	age (in years)	
		18 - 30	31 - 60
men	60	10700	10500
	65	11200	10800
	70	11700	11200
	75	12200	11600
	80	12700	12000
	85	13200	12400
	90	13700	12800
women	45	7700	8100
	50	8200	8300
	55	8700	8600
	60	9200	8900
	65	9700	9200
	70	10200	9500
	75	10700	9800

Source: *Recommended Dietary Intakes for use in Australia*, Australian Government Publishing Service, Canberra, 1991.

1) To convert to kCalories divide by 4.2

Table 2 **estimated energy expenditure in kJoules[1]/minute**

discipline	body weight (in kg)				
	50	60	70	80	90
running					
7 min/km	29	34	42	46	50
5.5 min/km	42	50	59	63	71
5 min/km	46	55	63	71	76
4.5 min/km	50	63	67	76	84
4 min/km	59	67	76	84	88
3.5 min/km	63	76	88	97	109
cycling					
15 km/hour	19	24	28	31	35
25 km/hour	34	41	47	53	60
30 km/hour	49	60	69	79	88
swimming					
freestyle	32	39	46	52	59

Source: Adapted from Melvin H. Williams, *Nutrition for fitness and sport*, Wm.C Brown Publishers, Iowa, 1988.

1) To convert kJoules to kCalories divide by 4.2

carbohydrate

Chapter 3 describes the energy systems in detail and highlights the importance of carbohydrate (CHO) as a superior fuel. Yet the body's capacity to store CHO is rather limited and this presents triathletes with a dilemma. CHO is stored in muscles and liver as glycogen. Muscle glycogen provides a ready source of energy during high intensity exercise, while liver glycogen acts to maintain normal levels of blood glucose, another important fuel. Intense daily training can rapidly exhaust glycogen reserves and decrease blood glucose levels resulting in fatigue and reduced performance **(see Fig. 2)**.

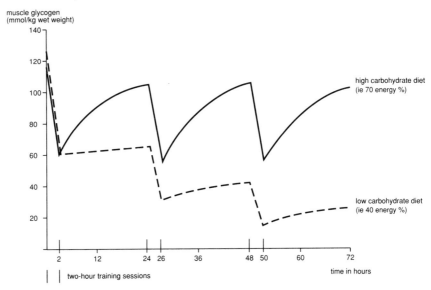

Fig. 2.

A high CHO diet maintains high muscle glycogen levels while a low CHO diet depletes glycogen stores rapidly.

Source: D.L. Costill and J.M. Miller, *International Journal of Sports Medicine*, 1:2-14, 1980.

For optimum glycogen stores a high daily CHO intake is essential and you should aim for the following levels:

daily carbohydrate requirements

6-8 grams/kg bodyweight	- recreational short course triathletes
9-10 grams/kg bodyweight	- middle and long course and competitive short course triathletes

This is equivalent to 60-70% of total energy. It is important to realise that it is not at all uncommon for triathletes to consume inadequate amounts of CHO, and it is a very useful exercise to estimate your current CHO intake and compare it with your estimated requirements.

Most triathletes should use primarily those CHO foods rich in other nutrients (vitamins, minerals and fibre), i.e. choose wholegrain breads and breakfast cereals, rice, pasta, muffins, fruit buns, potatoes and a wide range of fresh fruits and vegetables. It is best to moderate intake of the less nutritious CHO foods such as sugars, fruit juice, sweets, sports drinks, jams etc. as although they provide CHO they are low in additional nutrients. Those with very high CHO needs (500 grams or more per day) may need to consume more sugars as it can be uncomfortable to have such large quantities exclusively from complex CHO. **Table 3** gives CHO content of a variety of foods.

Table 3

carbohydrate counter

Each of these servings provides approximately 20 grams of carbohydrate

2 thin-medium slices bread	1 medium potato, kumara, parsnip or taro
$1^1/_2$ toast slice bread	$^1/_2$ cup yams
$^1/_2$ large breadroll, hamburger bun or fruit bun	$^2/_3$ cup sweet corn
1 small or $^1/_2$ large pitabread pocket	1 cup beetroot or broad beans
1 crumpet or English muffin	1 large apple, pear, orange or peach
4-6 crackers or crispbreads	1 medium banana
1 cup cooked rolled oats porridge (5 Tb raw)	2 large apricots or kiwifruit
2 Weetbix	4 dates
1 cup cornflakes, rice bubbles, shredded wheat or bran flakes	6 prunes
$^2/_3$ cup sultana bran	12 dried apricot halves
$^1/_3$ cup untoasted muesli (sweetened)	3 Tb sultanas or raisins
3 cups popcorn (plain)	200ml unsweetened fruit juice
$^1/_3$ cup cooked rice	400 ml milk
$^1/_2$ cup cooked pasta	300 ml plain, unsweetened yoghurt
4 plain sweet biscuits	150 ml fruit flavoured, sweetened yoghurt
1 scone	2 scoops icecream
1 muffin	1 can Exceed Sports Nutrition Supplement
1 muesli bar	75 ml Sustagen Sport (1 $^1/_2$ Tb powder)
1 cup cooked lentils, kidney beans or chick peas	1 Tb honey, jam, golden syrup or sugar
$^2/_3$ cup baked beans	2 Tb Milo
	200 ml cordial / soft drink
	200-300 ml sports drink

Source: *Diet 1 New Zealand*, NZ Food Composition Database 1992, (OCNZ '92)

protein

Athletes, especially those involved in strength sports, have argued for years that they need extra protein, yet research has only recently been able to back this claim. Triathletes need more protein primarily as there is an increased oxidation of amino acids (especially the branched chain ones) in endurance training which means that protein is used as an auxiliary fuel. Before you rush out to buy protein powders though, do realise that the increased amounts needed are easily obtained from the typical sports diet.

daily protein requirements

1.2-1. 6 g/kg bodyweight	- most triathletes
2 g/kg bodyweight	- adolescent triathletes

Table 4 gives protein content of a variety of foods.

Table 4

protein counter

Each of these servings provides approximately 15 grams of protein

50 g lean, cooked meat, chicken (skinned) or turkey	1 large milkshake
75 g lean, cooked mince	1 can Exeed Sports Nutrition Supplement
1 small fillet of fish, baked	125 ml Sustagen Sport (2 $^1/_2$ Tb powder)
75 g salmon or sardines (canned, in brine)	$^1/_3$ cup cooked soy beans
50 g tuna (canned, in brine)	1 cup cooked kidney or baked beans
2 large eggs	$^1/_2$ cup mixed nuts
400 ml milk	3 Tb peanut butter
60 g cheese (cheddar, 2 thick slices)	200g ($^2/_3$ cup) tofu
100 g ($^1/_2$ cup) cottage cheese	4 - 5 slices bread
300 ml yoghurt	3 cups cooked pasta or rice

Source: *Diet 1 New Zealand*, NZ Food Composition Database 1992, (OCNZ '92)

It is best to choose mostly low fat protein sources such as lean red meat; skinned poultry; fish; low fat milk, yoghurt and cheeses; pulses and tofu. Triathletes at risk from an inadequate protein intake include vegetarians who do not substitute meat adequately, those who avoid all dairy products, those on restricted kJoule diets and overzealous carbo gobblers who focus too much on CHO consumption.

fluids

Working muscles produce a lot of heat (in fact 75 percent of energy expended in exercise is released as heat) and to prevent heat stress to the body it needs to be removed efficiently. Sweat evaporation is the main avenue for heat dissipation. However sweating can induce large fluid losses which in turn will lead to overheating and decreased performance **(see Table 5)**. Individual sweat rates do vary between athletes and also depend on environmental conditions. During intense exercise in hot, humid weather up to 2 litres of fluid can be lost per hour. It is crucial that fluid intake matches output and training provides an excellent opportunity to evaluate your fluid balance. Body weight is a good indicator of fluid loss and weighing yourself before and after training (in light clothing and using the same scales) in a variety of situations (long-slow, short-fast, long-fast training in all disciplines; hot-humid, cool weather) gives you valuable information on your individual needs. A 1 kg weight loss indicates a fluid deficit of 1 litre. Your aim is to minimise training induced weight losses by taking fluids regularly through the day, during long training sessions (including swimming) and in amounts that are determined on the basis of body weight checks and urine production. (Producing liberal amounts of pale urine at frequent intervals is a sign of full hydration.) Keep in mind that thirst is not a good indicator of fluid requirements; in fact, it indicates the onset of dehydration. As caffeine (from coffee) and alcohol are diuretics, they can contribute to dehydration.

Table 5

physiological effects of fluid loss

fluid loss (% of total body weight)	physiological effect
2	Impaired temperature regulation but not athletic performance
3	Decreased muscular endurance
4 - 6	Decreased muscular strength
>6	Heat stress injuries
	Heat cramps
Increasing dehydration	Heat exhaustion
	Heat stroke
	Coma
	Death

vitamins

Many triathletes view vitamins as magical substances; i.e. you need to take them from a bottle! There is also a persistent belief that vitamins provide energy. Both are incorrect.

Vitamins do have important functions in the body and several are exercise related. Some of the B group of vitamins, for example, are involved in energy metabolism while others have a role in red blood cell formation. Still others contribute to protein synthesis and tissue repair. Although deficiency can adversely affect athletic performance, it is unlikely that you will develop a deficiency on a high energy and nutritious diet that includes plenty of whole grains and lots of fresh fruit and vegetables, especially the brightly coloured varieties. Taking vitamins in amounts beyond your requirements is not necessarily a good thing. Some of the available supplements are very potent and may cause adverse reactions, as results from some scientific trials have shown.

With regard to the belief that vitamins provide energy, the following explanation may help. CHO, protein and fat are the only energy yielding nutrients. Vitamins have a role in the processes whereby this energy is released. But they do not provide energy themselves.

There are some groups of triathletes who may be at risk from marginal vitamin status including those who follow restrictive weight reduction regimes, junk food addicts and women using oral contraceptives. These groups should be individually assessed and, where possible, the quality of diet maximised rather than supplementing with vitamin pills at random.

minerals

Minerals are another important group of essential nutrients. They form the hard bony structure of the body, are involved in chemical reactions and in regulating water balance, muscle contraction and nerve response. Many of the minerals are implicated in exercise training and two have been identified as being of particular importance to athletes. Both low iron and calcium can contribute to specific problems and will be discussed in some detail.

iron

As explained in Chapter 17, iron deficiency is fairly common amongst triathletes. Inadequate dietary intake and reduced iron absorption are contributing factors. Although a diagnosed iron deficiency requires supplementation, optimising diet is an essential preventative strategy. There are three issues to consider.

1. Dietary iron intake.
2. Iron absorption.
3. Iron loss from the body.

1. Iron intake: There are two forms of food iron, haem and non-haem iron. Haem iron is found in animal foods such as red meat (including liver and kidneys), chicken (especially the darker flesh) and some seafood (oysters, mussels, sardines). Non-haem iron is found in vegetable foods like whole grains, green and leafy vegetables, pulses, dried fruit, nuts, seeds and in eggs. Iron content of haem sources is generally higher than that of non-haem. Dietary intake of iron is related to total energy intake with high energy diets providing the most. Menstruating women require significantly more iron than men yet their energy requirement is lower and this explains in part the higher incidence of iron deficiency amongst female athletes. Recommended daily intake of iron for male and non-menstruating female triathletes is 7-17 mg, while menstruating female triathletes require between 16-23 mg. Those who have a high requirement for iron need to make optimum food choices by including haem iron foods in their daily diets. **Table 6** gives the iron content of a variety of foods.

2. Iron absorption: Haem iron is much better absorbed compared with non-haem. However, the presence of haem iron enhances the absorption of non-haem. Vitamin C enhances iron absorption also and it is important to include food sources of this vitamin at each meal. These include citrus, kiwi and berry fruits, fruit juices, and fresh vegetables such as capsicum, broccoli, Brussels sprouts, kale etc. Tannic acid found in tea reduces iron absorption as do polyphenols in coffee. It is best to avoid these beverages at mealtimes if you are prone to iron deficiency (have them one hour either side of meals and in moderate amounts only). Phytates in wheatbran (and foods containing bran) and oxalates in spinach and silverbeet also reduce iron absorption.

3. Iron loss: There are several avenues for potential iron loss, including in sweat, through gastrointestinal bleeding, red blood cell destruction as a result of continual pounding while running (footstrike haemolysis) and in women through menstruation.

When considering all these factors it is no surprise that athletes become iron deficient. It is therefore of prime importance that you eat plenty of iron rich foods every day and that you adopt strategies that maximise iron absorption.

Table 6.

iron counter

food			iron content (mg)
haem sources			
Cooked, lean red meat	-	100 g	4.3
Cooked liver	-	100 g	10.0
Liver pate	-	2 Tb (30 g)	2.8
Cooked chicken (dark flesh)	-	100 g	2.6
Cooked fish	-	100 g	0.4
Raw oysters	-	6	4.5
Cooked mussels	-	$^2/_3$ cup (100 g)	7.7
Sardines	-	1 can (100 g)	2.9
non-haem sources			
Bran cereal	-	1 cup (45 g)	3.8
Wholemeal bread	-	2 slices	1.0
Cooked spinach	-	1 cup	6.7
Cooked green peas	-	1 cup	2.0
Cooked broccoli	-	1 cup	1.6
Dried apricots	-	$^1/_2$ cup	2.8
Sultanas	-	$^1/_2$ cup	1.4
Baked beans, kidney beans	-	1 cup	3.8
Mixed nuts	-	$^1/_2$ cup	0.9
Boiled eggs	-	2	2.2
Tofu	-	$^1/_2$ cup (130 g)	7.0

Source: *Diet 1 New Zealand*, NZ Food Composition Database 1992, (OCNZ '92)

calcium

Calcium is the major bone mineral and is important in achieving peak bone mass. It is essential for everyone to have an adequate intake of calcium to support bone building, a process which is completed at age 30-35. As explained in some detail in Chapter 17, amenorrhoeic (i.e. non-menstruating) females may develop low bone density levels and this increases their requirement for calcium. Calcium is, however, only one dietary factor to consider in athletic amenorrhoea. Inadequate energy intake, very low fat consumption, and vegetarian diets (especially the absence of red meat) are also associated with this condition. It is important that all dietary aspects are considered in the management of amenorrhoea including an increased calcium intake. The recommended daily intake for calcium is:

1000 mg per day	-	adolescent females
800 mg per day	-	adult females
1200 mg per day	-	amenorrhoeic athletes

Table 7 gives calcium content of a variety of foods.

Table 7

calcium counter

food			calcium content (mg)
Trim milk	-	200 ml	302
Homogenised milk	-	200 ml	239
Plain unsweetened yoghurt	-	200 g	236
Fruit flavoured yoghurt	-	200 g	224
Icecream (reduced energy)	-	1 cup	217
Cheese (cheddar, edam)	-	20 g (1 slice)	150
Cottage cheese	-	$^1/_2$ cup (100 g)	76
Salmon (with bones)	-	100 g	93
Sardines	-	100 g	550
Baked beans	-	1 cup	121
Soy milk (So Good)	-	200 ml	232
Tofu	-	$^1/_2$ cup (130 g)	137
Sesame seeds	-	2 Tb	22
Mixed nuts	-	$^1/_2$ cup	28

Source: *Diet 1 New Zealand*, NZ Food Composition Database 1992, (OCNZ '92)

putting it all together

The final step towards meeting your dietary goals is to plan for everyday meals and snacks. This section provides guidelines on meal planning and gives examples of suitable high energy meals and snacks.

Guidelines

- Eat often and aim to have at least three main meals each day. It is not unusual for triathletes to snack continuously and have less defined meals and this is no problem so long as the sum total adds up to the right kind and amount of food. This grazing type of pattern tends to occur especially when training more than once a day.

- Plan each meal (and snack) around a staple CHO food such as bread, breakfast cereal, rice, pasta, potato, pulses or a combination. For additional CHO eat fruits and/or vegetables with most meals. These also make excellent snacks.

- All main meals and at least some of your snack type meals need to include a source of protein. This may range from milk or yoghurt on cereals or in milk shakes, to chicken, eggs, lean meat, humus or tuna in sandwiches through to lean meat, fish, poultry, pulses or tofu with your dinner.

- Minimise added fat from margarine, oil and butter. Use light spreads only on bread and cook in a non-stick frypan, grill, microwave or roast without using fat. Reserve high fat snacks such as chocolate, crisps, pastries, pies, cakes etc. for occasional treats.

- Include drinks of water and/or fruit juice with meals and snacks.

- Planning meals is made easier when doing grocery shopping regularly (weekly or fortnightly) and writing a shopping list by checking through your fridge and pantry.

meal and snack ideas

breakfast

* Untoasted muesli with low fat yoghurt and fruit
* Rolled oat porridge with Trim milk, sultanas and brown sugar
* Fruit muffins, topped with jam
* Scrambled eggs on wholemeal toast

Include fresh fruit and/or fruit juice.

lunch

* Salmon and salad wholemeal sandwiches
* Pita bread filled with chicken and tomato, shredded lettuce, sprouts and cucumber
* Chick pea salad, mixed with salad vegetables, low fat dressing and served on a lettuce leaf
* Corn and potato chowder with wholemeal bread rolls

Include fresh fruit and/or fruit juice

dinner

* Stuffed baked potato (mushroom & cheese) with baked fillet of fish and a variety of vegetables
* Stir fry rice and vegetables with strips of beef schnitzel
* Spaghetti bolognaise (low fat sauce) and salad
* Kidney bean casserole with sauteed vegetables and a spicy tomato sauce

Include fruit juice or water

desserts

* Fresh fruit salad and yoghurt
* Cereal and low fat milk
* Rice pudding and sultanas
* Pancakes, filled with fruit compote

high energy snacks

* Muffins
* Scones
* Fruit loaf
* Fruit or iced buns

* Instant noodles
* Popcorn
* Muesli bars (low fat)
* Cereals and yoghurt or milk

* Crumpets
* Fresh fruit
* Dried fruit
* Sports Bars (Exceed, Power, Energiser Bars)

* Milk shakes
* Yoghurt
* Meal supplement (Exceed Sports Nutrition Supplement or Sustagen)

competition nutrition

Putting the right dietary programme in place during training is laying the foundation for maximum race performance. Dietary manipulation at the time of competition is like icing the cake; it is a small, yet crucial part of achieving your dietary goals. What you plan to do in competition needs to be tried in training; there is no room for surprises on the day! It is a good idea to plan your diet well in advance of race day, more so when you compete away from home. It gives you the confidence that everything is under control and allows you to concentrate on other last minute things that need to be done, like checking your bike etc.

There are three stages to consider at this time: pre-competition, race menu and post-race. Each of these stages may need to be approached differently depending on whether you are doing a short, middle or full course triathlon.

pre-competition

This phase includes the three days prior to your race and the hours before. For middle and long course races you want to carbohydrate load. For a sprint or short distance this is not necessary although you may want to consider it for the main race of your season. The pre-race meal is similar for all distances.

Your objectives at this particular stage are to maximise muscle glycogen stores (carbohydrate loading), maximise liver glycogen reserves (pre-race meal), optimise hydration levels and electrolyte balance and allow for a fairly empty stomach at the start (to prevent gastrointestinal problems).

carbohydrate loading

Carbohydrate loading is the technique by which muscle glycogen levels are increased beyond levels normally achieved through a high CHO diet. The original regime included a depletion phase during which glycogen levels are depleted (through hard training and a low CHO diet) before they are maximised through tapering and increased CHO consumption. This approach tended to contribute to injuries and feelings of lethargy and tiredness and it has been found that high glycogen levels can equally be achieved by following the second phase only. The current advice is to follow an appropriate tapering programme and rest on the day before your race while increasing CHO consumption to 9-10 grams per kg body weight (85 percent of total energy) for the three days prior to the race. Although you may consume this amount of CHO whilst training you will now store up more of it as glycogen. When training less your total energy needs are decreased yet you do need to consume maximum CHO. It follows that the consumption of other energy foods has to be reduced. Fat intake should be very minimal while protein consumption needs to be moderate. This obviously does not fit with the usual CHO loading of large plates of pasta smothered in meat sauce and topped with lots of cheese! Proper carbohydrate loading does require some creative thinking and planning. **Table 8** gives some ideas on suitable meals. When eating minimal fat and less protein you will get hungry a lot more often. This is because CHO foods digest relatively quickly. Make sure you satisfy your appetite. To optimise hydration and because glycogen binds water in the muscle, you need extra fluid. For convenience you may combine fluid and CHO by drinking more fruit juice or using a sports drink or high CHO drink **(Tables 9 and 10)**. Due to the increased water content of the muscles, you will put on some weight while loading and in fact this is a means to check you have loaded successfully. You can expect to put on up to 2 kg. Avoid all alcohol in the days leading up to the race.

Table 8.

carbohydrate loading meal ideas

breakfast

1. Fruit salad topped with low fat yoghurt and low fat muesli

2. Pancakes (no added butter, Trim milk) cooked in a non stick pan and filled with fruit compote

3. Toast (no margarine), topped with jam, honey or banana

    Include a drink of fruit juice or high CHO beverage

lunch

1. Breadrolls, pitabread or sandwiches (no butter or margarine) filled with cottage cheese, skinned chicken, turkey or salmon/tuna and salad greens

2. Pasta salad (use low fat commercial dressing), mixed with diced vegetables and chicken or tuna

3. Soup (potato, kumara, minestrone, corn) served with unbuttered breadrolls

    Include fresh fruit and a drink of fruit juice or high CHO beverage

dinner

1. Baked potatoes, topped with cottage cheese (blend in food processor with some lemon juice, salt and pepper) and chives. High CHO vegetables such as corn, peas, beetroot, yam. Baked or microwaved fillet of fish
    Fresh fruit salad and yoghurt

2. Stir fry rice, vegetables and marinated tofu, cooked in a non stick pan.
    Cereal and Trim milk

3. Pasta with tomato sauce (homemade or bought) and diced, skinned chicken. Kumara salad (low fat dressing).
    Creamed rice and fruit

    Include a drink of fruit juice or high CHO beverage

snacks

* crumpets and golden syrup	* instant noodles
* muffins/scones and jam	* sports energy bars
* fresh or dried fruit	* fruit buns

pre-race meal

This meal is similar for all race distances. Aim to have your pre-race meal two to four hours prior to the start. If the start is very early and you are not keen to get up you can use a liquid meal replacement such as Exceed Sports Nutrition Supplement or Sustagen 1.5 to 2 hours prior to the start. These products will optimise nutrition but are low residue and digest quickly. They may also be of benefit for those who find it difficult to take in solid food at this time. If you opt for eating ordinary foods it is important that these are high in CHO, easy to digest and low in fat, fibre and protein. Choosing your food is a matter of blending the theoretical principles with your own preferences and previous experiences. White or brown bread, crumpets, English or other low fibre muffins topped with jam, honey or banana (no butter or margarine), light cereals such as cornflakes or rice bubbles with Trim milk or low fat yoghurt and fruit or low fat and low fibre pancakes are good choices. Include several cups of fruit juice or sports drink. While you get ready for the race carry a drink bottle with you and continue to drink, especially if it is going to be a hot day.

race menu

Your ultimate goal is for your race menu to contribute to the best possible performance.

The objectives are to avoid glycogen depletion and disturbances in electrolyte balance, and minimise dehydration (**see Chapter 17**). Your menu very much depends on the type of race and also on your past experiences. In sprint and short distances the main threat is dehydration so you need to take fluids. Water will be adequate in most situations. Some triathletes do prefer using a carbohydrate replacement drink and particularly in your most important short course races this may be of benefit. In the middle and long distance races dehydration, energy depletion and disturbed electrolyte balance all pose threats to your wellbeing and performance. This is particularly the case in hot and humid conditions. The ultimate triathlon, the Hawaiian Ironman, for example, places incredible stresses on your fluid and fuel reserves.

A planned and aggressive regime of regular fluid and carbohydrate ingestion will greatly enhance your ability to race well. There are several key factors to consider:

- Knowing what your likely requirements are, based on the information provided in this chapter, your previous experience and experimentation in training.
- Planning your regime in detail, down to when to take fluids and food, which type and how much, yet remaining flexible enough to make adjustments if necessary.
- Finding out which beverages and what food are made available by the race

organisers and how frequently.
- Anticipating weather conditions where possible and allowing time to acclimatise.

State of the art knowledge suggests that fluid consumption should be in the order of 600-1200 ml per hour to prevent or minimise dehydration. 600 ml will be adequate under cool conditions especially for those triathletes who do not perspire heavily, while 1200 ml may be required in hot and humid conditions and for those who sweat profusely. The stomach can empty up to 1 litre of fluid per hour comfortably. Keep in mind that in extreme circumstances you may lose up to 2 litres of fluid per hour. Start drinking as early as possible, i.e. in the swim-bike transition, and continue right through the race. Cold fluids help cool the body and large volumes are emptied from the stomach at a faster rate. This means that it may be useful to take in a large volume initially, approximately 400 ml (or as much as feels comfortable) which is topped up every 10 minutes.

The important issues in CHO consumption are the concentration, amount, type and form in which it is taken. Concentrations of 5-10 percent CHO (i.e. 50-100 grams per litre) are well tolerated. An intake of 60 grams CHO per hour (or 1 gram per kg body weight) is the recommended amount to prevent glycogen depletion and low blood glucose levels, however some male triathletes feel they need more than this, so experiment. Glucosepolymers (hydrolysed cornstarch or malto dextrins), sucrose (table sugar) and glucose are all suitable. When using fairly high concentrations of around 10 per cent, glucosepolymers may however have a faster stomach emptying rate. Small amounts of fructose are often added to sports drinks to enhance flavour. Large amounts should be avoided as fructose is not as effective as other carbohydrates in providing extra fuel and large amounts may cause diarrhoea. Finally, it is best to take carbohydrates in liquid form as fluids are processed through the gastrointestinal tract faster than solids and are less likely to cause discomfort.

In an effort to avoid disturbances in electrolyte balance and because sodium enhances fluid and glucose absorption from the gut, sodium also needs to be incorporated in your drinks. Although there is no agreement at present as to the optimum sodium level, the likely amount is between 10-30 mmol per litre of fluid (i.e. 230-690 mg sodium which is equivalent to 1/4 teaspoon of salt). Including sodium also decreases the risk of water intoxication **(see Chapter 17)**. Several sports drinks containing CHO and sodium are now available and they can be used as the base of your race menu. **Table 9** gives an overview of available CHO drinks. It is a good idea to experiment with several and choose the one that suits you best. Taste preference is an important consideration as studies have clearly shown that athletes are more likely to meet their fluid and CHO requirements if they enjoy the taste of their drink. Many triathletes drink water as well as a sports drink, both for a change and because CHO drinks tend to make your mouth feel sticky. This is fine provided you also take sufficient CHO. In a full course triathlon most triathletes like to eat as well as drink. Theoretically you can meet your needs using a carbohydrate drink. However, an empty stomach can feel quite uncomfortable and that is the main reason for taking solids. The sports bars that are now available are suitable for this purpose and other high carbohydrate foods such as bananas, dried fruit, low fat cookies, white bread sandwiches, low fibre fruit loaves and muffins are all good choices. Once again, make sure you experiment with different regimes in training. The following guidelines summarise dietary strategies during middle and long distance events.

- Use a CHO replacement beverage of your choice as your base nutrition.

- Start drinking early and continue at frequent intervals right through the race.

- Take in a large volume initially (approximately 400 ml or as much as feels comfortable) and top this up every 10-15 minutes at a rate of 600-1200 ml total fluid per hour.

- Take in approximately 60 grams carbohydrate per hour or 1 gram per kg body weight using a sports drink with a 5-10% concentration.

- Choose a beverage with a sodium content of 10-30 mmol per litre.

- Choose a nice tasting beverage.

- Where possible choose cold fluids.

- Supplement your sports drink with water if you wish.

- Eat moderate amounts of food if you wish, primarily during the cycle section, and choose high carbohydrate foods with little or no fat, protein or fibre.

Table 9.   **carbohydrate-electrolyte replacement drinks**
comparison per 1 litre (4 cups) of made-up drink

name	CHO content (g)	CHO type	sodium (mg[1])
Exceed Fluid and Energy Replacement	68	Glucosepolymer, Fructose	200
Replace	76	Glucose, Glucosepolymer, Fructose	210
Gatorade	64	Sucrose, Glucose	440
Sustalyte	60	Dextrose (glucose)	200
Carboblast	76	Glucosepolymer, Glucose, Fructose	263
Squeezy	100	Glucosepolymer, Fructose	-
Enduro booster	97	Glucosepolymer, Fructose	-

1) To convert sodium to mmol (or mEq) divide by 23

post-race
Even if you have looked after your fluid and carbohydrate needs during a race, there is likely to be a certain degree of dehydration and almost certainly low glycogen levels. If these problems are not dealt with quickly your rate of recovery will be reduced. This in turn will affect your ability to pick up training again. Especially when racing frequently and after middle and long distance races when

you get severely depleted, your nutritional strategies post-race are very important. Rehydration is enhanced by continuing to take fluids straight after the race and avoiding alcohol for some time. Blood sugar levels and muscle and liver glycogen stores will be replenished quicker and more completely when taking CHO within an hour of finishing. You need 1-2 grams of carbohydrate per kg bodyweight at this particular time. Sugars appear to be more effective in glycogen repletion immediately post race compared with the nutritious CHO's. As you may not be hungry, it is most convenient to use a carbohydrate beverage. This can either be your race drink or a high carbohydrate drink **(Table 10)**. These drinks also contain electrolytes. A similar amount of carbohydrate should be taken between two and four hours post race. At this stage you are probably ready for a meal. Continue to take fluids until you start passing clear urine at regular intervals. Those who compete in a full course triathlon may find they are very hungry for several days post race. This is not surprising when one considers how much energy is required to finish such an event and the extent of depletion which is likely to occur. Satisfy your appetite, even if it may seem excessive.

Table 10.

high carbohydrate drinks
comparison per 1 litre (4 cups) of made-up drink

name	CHO content (g)	CHO type	sodium (mg[1])
Exceed High Carbohydrate Source	236	Glucosepolymer, Sucrose, Glucose	470
Carbo-Energy	235	Glucosepolymer, Glucose, Fructose	675
Carboplex	148	Glucosepolymer, Glucose, Fructose	-

1) To convert sodium to mmol (or mEq) divide by 23.

a weighty issue

Triathletes, especially at the elite level, tend to be characterised by their leanness and upper body muscle development. Low body fat levels are an advantage in a sport where speed counts. The upper body development is a result of swim training and indeed helps swimming performance. Too much bulk, though, is a disadvantage as it may slow you down in running and cycling. Although changes in body shape and size do occur as a result of training, we are also born with our own unique body shape which is genetically determined. This does not just mean that some of us are naturally taller than others. It also causes some of us to be more muscular or to carry more body fat than others. Within what is realistically possible, it is a definite advantage for triathletes to have low body fat levels. Most of us assess our body weight by using scales. The problem is that total weight is pretty meaningless and does not tell you how much fat you are carrying. Therefore, additional methods are required. The simplest and most available test involves measuring skin folds at various sites of the body using a set of callipers. Generally body fat is expressed as a percentage, however the prediction equations used to calculate percentage fat are not particularly accurate and there is now a trend to use total sum of skin folds as the measure. To get a reasonable idea of fat distribution it is best to measure a relatively large number of skin folds, i.e. seven for women and eight for men. Although we do not have figures on ideal body fat for triathletes it seems reasonable for women to aim for a sum of skin folds of between 50 and 80 mm while the figure for men lies between 35 and 60 mm. It is best to use this method as a comparative one, i.e. comparing your own body fat levels over time. The 7/8 skin fold sites used in this particular method are triceps, subscapular, calf, biceps, supra-iliac, abdomen, thigh and in men the axilla. It is crucial that a skilled person measures your skin folds and it is a definite advantage being measured by the same person on subsequent tests.

Training will go a long way towards reducing your body fat if you have excessive amounts, however dietary modification may also be necessary. It can be tricky to modify diet in a way that allows you to lose weight while still maintaining a high energy and carbohydrate intake to support training. The following guidelines will help you achieve both goals.

- Avoid fad diets as these are often severely restricted and lack essential nutrients.

- Reduce total daily energy intake by approximately 2000 kJoules (500 kCalories) to achieve a reduction in body fat of approximately $^1/_2$ kg per week.

- Maintain a high carbohydrate diet and use primarily the nutritious carbohydrates for maximum value. Cut down on sugars.

- Minimise intake of fat. This is your main avenue for cutting kiloJoules.

- Avoid alcohol.

- As reducing energy intake increases protein requirements, make sure you get adequate amounts of protein (choose low fat sources) but there is no advantage in over-consumption of protein.

- Drink plenty of fluids, especially water.

- If your energy intake is 6000 kJoules or more per day and you follow the above guidelines your intake of essential vitamins and minerals is likely to be adequate.

- If your energy consumption is less you may require a supplement. You should discuss this with your dietitian.

- Be realistic about the time frame you set yourself. Reducing body fat levels takes time, it does not happen overnight.

- Large weight losses over a short period of time are caused by a reduction in fluid and lean body mass as well as fat and this is to be avoided at all costs.

vegetarian eating

Vegetarian diets are now firmly established in Western societies and many triathletes have adopted this way of eating. It is important to establish your reasons for being a vegetarian. If it is because you believe it is a healthier way of eating or your triathlon hero follows it you will have to think again. Although over-consumption of meat is not good, lean meat does provide very important nutrients. First there is the protein. Animal protein found in meat, fish, chicken, eggs and dairy products contains all essential amino acids (those amino acids the body cannot manufacture itself) as opposed to plant protein such as pulses, tofu, nuts, seeds, cereal foods and vegetables which lack one particular amino acid. When relying exclusively on plant protein you need to know how to combine the different sources for the right balance of amino acids. Secondly, red meat is very high in iron and zinc. Iron deficiency has been discussed in detail and zinc is another important mineral related to exercise. Zinc levels in the New Zealand soil are low and this combined with a vegetarian diet may contribute to a zinc deficiency. Vitamin B12 is another nutrient found in meat, fish and chicken and many athletes believe they have an increased requirement for B12.

The real issue is one of choosing the right amount and type of meat. Consuming lean meat 3-4 times a week in quantities of 100-150 grams optimises your intake of essential nutrients and contributes to good health.

If, however, you are following a vegetarian diet for other reasons such as religion or because you have strong feelings about the killing of animals, then it is a matter of making appropriate substitutions for the lack of animal foods in your diet. In this case you should invest in a good vegetarian recipe book that includes information on nutritional principles.

16

mental attitude

Training and nutrition provide the basis for triathlon performance. Mental attitude decides the performance edge. The more competitive the triathlete, the more important mental attitude becomes. The difference in performance between equally talented, trained and fit athletes is in the mind.

It is intriguing to try and find out what motivates us to do triathlons. This will be different for every individual. The triathlon is generally considered to be somewhat excessive by the general population. The commitment and discipline required to finish an event comfortably, particularly when competing, is significant, especially for the working family person.

Is it related to childhood traumas or is it just embedded in our personality? Probably a bit of both. Most humans have an inborn desire to achieve; some have this urge stronger than others. Triathletes can be placed in the "high achievers" category. This is probably why the triathlon attracts so many successful business people and professionals.

The competitive triathlete is not only motivated to finish the event comfortably, but at the same time is aiming to achieve a maximum performance level. Competitive triathletes, like any competitive athletes, are motivated by desire (to do well) or by fear (of failure). Initially in a triathlete's career the desire to do well will overrule the fear, but once established the chance, and therefore the fear, of failure increases. This has been especially applicable to the triathlon which has developed so fast.

In the early years of the sport 80 percent of triathletes would just enter a race to finish, with 20 percent being competitive. Now those figures are reversed. The champions of the early 80s had it relatively easy. Not many have survived as they could not handle the pressure of so many young competitive triathletes threatening their positions. This despite the fact that many of those established triathletes had not reached their maximum potential. The ones who have survived have learnt to deal with the competitiveness and have accepted the fact of defeat. Most are still doing surprisingly well. The difference has been their mental adjustment. At top level there is a magnification of desire and fear brought on by exposure from the media (including expectations), involvement of money and the nature of racing particularly at national representative level.

All people are egotists. Sportspeople more so, and nowhere does this apply better than in the triathlon. The egotistical part of being a triathlete is essential for success, but can seriously interfere with social and work activities. Finding the balance in the triathlon does not only apply to the three disciplines, it also applies to the balance of life. This chapter on mental strategies for triathlon performance is aimed at the more competitive triathlete who strives for optimum performance.

mental attitude of successful elite triathletes

Research has shown that successful participants in different sports use similar psychological strategies for mental preparation before and during competition. No specific research in this area has been done on triathletes. From general results from other sports, findings can be applied specifically to the triathlon.

The following is an attempt to apply the psychological profile of successful elite athletes specifically to the triathlete.

psychological profile of the successful elite triathlete

- Ability to concentrate on a single goal during training. This applies to peaking for major events. To be single minded in training towards the one performance goal is one of the most essential elements of peaking for a particular race.

- Ability to put more effort into racing than training. Some triathletes show tremendous ability in training, but never seem to emulate this during competition. They are the champions of training.

- Ability to perform up to expectations and to judge competitive ability. This includes being able to set realistic goals and achieve them with confidence.

- Ability to plan a detailed competitive strategy. Careful planning of training and racing strategies is essential for achieving optimum results.

- Ability to maintain composure when things go wrong. Many things can go wrong during a triathlon, including adverse weather conditions, equipment failure and unexpected obstacles during a race. The successful triathlete is not phased by these, but rather sees them as a challenge.

- Frequent use of mental imagery (visualisation). Top triathletes intuitively practise upcoming races in their minds many times, often in minute details in the period leading up to the race.

- Ability to adjust pre-competitive arousal to an optimum level. This applies to the pre-competitive state of mind, which should be a controlled level of nervousness and tension.

- Ability to control composure before competition. Many elite triathletes have feelings relating to a loss of confidence at some stage in the time leading up to a major event. The ability to control this is crucial for success.

- Ability to compete well under all conditions, familiar or unfamiliar.

- Ability to concentrate on performance without worrying about other competitors.

- Ability to be independent of a coach, especially close to race time. More so than in any other sport, triathletes are very much on their own during training, before and during competition.

- Ability to save oneself for a good finishing effort. Most competitive athletes prefer to stamp their authority on an event from the beginning. This is not always appropriate in the triathlon where the race is often decided during the second half of the last event which is the run.

- Ability to concentrate on a strategy throughout the race, to concentrate on technique when tired and to handle the pressures in the final stages of a close competition.

- Ability to produce a maximum effort even when beaten.

- Ability to learn from each race and modify racing strategies accordingly.

mental preparation for training and competition

Through practice, mental attitude to training and competition can be improved! For very few triathletes the abilities mentioned in the above list come naturally. Most successful elite triathletes work hard at their mental skills like they work on their training and nutritional strategies. The first step is to recognise mental strengths and weaknesses, followed by the second step of working on the weak areas.

Following are some training techniques which can be used to improve skills in different areas of mental attitude.

motivation

Motivation is the general level of arousal to action in an individual. For the competitive triathlete motivation has to come from within. Compared with other sports, there are few competitors who need to be motivated. Many need to be slowed down or they need help to have their motivation and energy channelled into appropriate training, nutritional and psychological techniques. This is where the role of the coach comes in. For the competitive triathlete motivation goes back to why they are doing triathlons. This can be different for every competitor, centred somewhere between past life experiences and personality characteristics. This has been discussed in the introduction to this chapter.

A distinction needs to be made between the competitive triathlete and triathletes who take part purely for health and fitness reasons. This is probably the most healthy and sensible way to be involved in the sport. Beginners are different from experienced triathletes and often do need encouragement and motivation particularly if they have no past exercise experience. Preparation for one event can be daunting, let alone three. This category has a high drop out rate. Encouragement can be given in different forms.

1. Organised group sessions under professional guidance are a very effective way of achieving compliance to a training regime. Group sessions can also be an excellent motivater for the more serious triathlete during times of hard training.

2. Assistance with the right choice of equipment.

3. The availability of short, fun, triathlons over gentle courses, which are easily achievable for most; e.g. women's-only triathlons have been hugely successful in motivating women into the sport, although many do not last.

4. Organised social activities, e.g. through triathlon clubs.

goal setting

The most common error made by many triathletes is that they only set long term goals, e.g. the beginner whose goal is to compete in the Hawaiian Ironman or the local junior club champ who wants to become the World Champion. For goal setting to work, it is more effective to break it down into short term goals and also to concentrate on performance orientated goals (e.g. technique, personal best times in the three disciplines etc.). Outcome goals (e.g. placing in a race) are too dependent on factors outside your control, e.g. other competitors, weather conditions etc.

The following is a summary of how to improve goal setting skills.

- Set realistic goals. Setting goals that are initially too high will undermine your motivation. Especially early on in your career and training, set goals which you know you can achieve comfortably.

- Avoid setting goals which are beyond your direct control (outcome related goals). Focus on goals which are related to your own performance (performance related goals).

- Set long term goals as this is good for motivation. Realise that short term goals are there to help you to achieve your long term goals.

- In general, put your emphasis on the short term goals (days, weeks, months) rather than long term goals (months to years). Daily short term goals include simple things like being on time at training sessions, doing quality training, improving technique etc.

- Break your short term goals down into single items, rather than an overall performance, e.g. the three different disciplines, mental skills, nutrition etc.

- Be prepared to adjust your goals as you go along. Goals need to be flexible to allow for unexpected obstacles like injuries and other commitments. This attitude will minimise frustration and enhance performance.

- Avoid the word "must" when setting goals (e.g. "I must win this race or otherwise I have failed"). This will lead to a loss of confidence in your own beliefs.

- Remember that goal setting does not only apply to physical training, but also to mental skill development, e.g. positive thinking, visualisation, relaxation and focus control.

The outcome of goal setting depends on: how realistic your goals are; how committed you are to reaching your goals; how flexible you are in adjusting your goals; and how much you believe in your ability to reach your goals.

Goal setting, done properly, can be very effective and satisfying.

anxiety and arousal

Before competition, triathletes tend to become increasingly anxious, leading to pre-competitive arousal. Pre-competitive anxiety can either be constructive or destructive depending on the nature of the accompanying thoughts which can be irrelevant, self orientated or task orientated. Self orientated thoughts are the most harmful as they take the form of worry and self doubt. Irrelevant thoughts often lead to a state of under arousal and under preparedness. Task orientated thoughts are most likely to result in an optimum arousal level.

The triathlete who has mostly self orientated thoughts will benefit most from professional help from a sports psychologist. The concept of arousal is shown in Fig. 1.

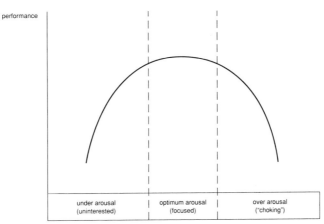

Fig. 1.

It has been found that athletes perform best when they are in the mid range of the curve (optimum arousal level). Inadequate or excessive arousal levels lead to reduced performance.

The two frequently used techniques to control arousal are autogenic training and thought controlling techniques.

Autogenic training concentrates on the functions of the muscles, the central nervous system and the mind. This is practised by lying in a relaxed position and imagining that your limbs are becoming warmer and heavier. Once this has been achieved you repeat your own personal autogenic phrase, e.g. I feel strong, focused and confident. If this is done repetitively it will result in an arousal response which is in accordance with the autogenic phrase.

The thought controlling technique is targeted at recognising and eliminating negative thoughts. This can be done by replacing them with positive thoughts and self statements by focusing on the task ahead.

focusing

Focusing is the uninterrupted connection between the athlete and his task (performance). When focused in sport you are aware only of things relating to your performance. Focusing can be practised by tuning in to your body and body movements when training and competing. This will result in an awareness of key feelings when things go well or poorly. Recognising key feelings when things go well will enable you to recall them at times of adversity. This will help you to refocus. Focusing is about controlling irrelevant and distracting thoughts during practice and competition and replacing them with task orientated and positive thoughts.

Worry is one of the threats to focus before or during a race. The ability to shut out worrying thoughts of self-doubt and replace them with positive thoughts on performance is crucial. This can be done by focusing on simple things like technique, your breathing or your race strategy. Self talk also helps to retain focus.

Focusing, like goal setting, needs to concentrate on performance rather than outcome.

Studies of marathon runners have found that elite runners are completely absorbed in their performance, called associative thinking. They focus on staying relaxed, feeling strong, their technique and breathing patterns etc. Non-elite runners, however, tend to think more about other things unrelated to their performance. This is called disassociative thinking. The tougher the going the more associative thinking (focusing) is required to stay competitive.

visualisation or mental imagery

Many athletes intuitively use mental imagery when preparing for races. Mental imagery is a powerful tool for achieving maximum performance. In the triathlon it especially applies to improving technique and racing performance. Practising in the mind what needs to be practised during training and racing makes the outcome more effective. For example, swimming is technically the most difficult discipline in the triathlon. Repetitive stroke corrections made in the mind will contribute to improved technique in the water. Serious triathletes should go through a race in their minds several times prior to competition. They should visualise the course, possible weather conditions, different race strategies, transitions etc. Although they will be aware of other athletes, the focus during mental imagery will be mainly on their own performance. This practice will prepare them for situations that can develop during a race. Different situations will then not come as a complete surprise, they have at least been practised in the mind.

The technique of visualisation can be improved and perfected through frequent practice.

relaxation and activation

Athletes tend to perform poorly more often because they are too tense or too anxious than too relaxed. To find the balance between tension and relaxation is the key to optimum mental performance. Different relaxation techniques are available to assist the athlete in reaching the optimum level of mental arousal. The first step in controlling your feelings of anxiety is to recognise the signs. Everybody responds differently. Some athletes simply get "choked up", others get headaches, violent diarrhoea or abdominal pains.

different techniques for relaxation include :

1. Focusing on relaxing different muscle groups

2. Focusing on breathing deeply, slowly and easily

3. Focusing on visualising calming situations, e.g. being on a nice beach with the sun setting on the horizon over a smooth sea, waves gently washing onto the beach

4. Focusing on physically relaxing activities, e.g. massage, listening to music, being with friends or being by yourself in a natural setting, a warm bath etc.

5. Practising key words which help you to relax, e.g. "relax" or "loose"

6. Combinations of the above

Relaxation techniques usually result in the slowing of bodily functions, e.g. lowering of heart rate, slowing of breathing and easing of muscle tension. They also result in psychological relaxation with thoughts shifting from worry to confidence and calmness. Relaxation needs to be practised under controlled conditions so it is easily recalled in times of stress and tension. Relaxation strategies are very individual and only experimenting will enable you to find which is the most effective strategy for you.

Activation/stimulation is less often required before competition, but might be needed before practice sessions and during the latter stages of racing when fatigue sets in. One way of coping with fatigue during races is to shift the focus away from the awareness of fatigue towards improving your performance, e.g. maintaining technique, power, strength etc. Alternatively, remind yourself of your goal and the importance of achieving it. Activation before competition, if required, can be achieved by heightening your awareness of the upcoming event as well as concentrating on becoming more active and intense, e.g. through a more vigorous warm up.

Getting activated for practices is more often required when time trialing and during periods of hard training. Setting specific training goals will help while also reminding you of your long term goals. Alternatively, you can compete against other athletes in training which can be highly stimulating. However, care has to be taken that the training does not evolve into an actual race.

controlling your emotions

Successful triathletes are able to control their emotions. They are able to channel these into their performance during training and racing. They have an ability to change from a state of negative thinking to positive thinking. These are the athletes who respond well to setbacks.

To balance the three disciplines in training as well as life in general can be difficult. Minor upsets like problems at home, equipment failure or niggling injuries can have disastrous consequences if related emotions cannot be controlled.

The most common emotions when things go wrong are disappointment, anger and frustration or combinations of these. The ability to control those emotions by quickly turning to positive thinking, refocusing and, where necessary, resetting goals, will significantly minimise any potential damage. Finishing a race well following the setback of a puncture, rather than withdrawing, can still give you tremendous personal satisfaction.

Reacting to errors and setbacks can be learnt like any other skill and it is often the more experienced athlete who has a cunning ability to salvage what for bystanders or less experienced athletes looks like a hopeless situation. Naturally, the best way to deal with setbacks during training and racing is to try and prevent them. This can be done by careful planning and preparation as well as by using reliable equipment. If, despite this, something unforeseen still occurs (e.g. being stopped by a train during a race), the more positive and constructive the response (e.g. after this short rest I should be able to catch up, so that is what I will focus on), the less likely it is to affect overall performance.

17

medical matters

A whole book could be written on medical factors related to the triathlon. In this chapter we will restrict ourselves to practical aspects of the more common medical problems encountered in the triathlon. The emphasis will be on prevention as the individual triathlete will be more interested in preventing illness and injury rather than having existing symptoms healed.

The threat of injury and overtraining is one of the limiting factors in how hard we can train. Months of careful preparation can be severely disrupted by injury or illness. Once symptoms have been established, there is frustratingly little the athlete can do to speed recovery except seek help from a health professional who has an interest in sports medicine. Remember that not all health professionals are sympathetic towards clients who suffer from problems relating to fitness and training. Athletes can receive inappropriate advice such as "have a rest", or "give it up".

Training for triathlons means exposure to stress, both physical and mental, and it is likely that most triathletes will have their training interrupted at least once a year through illness or injury. The serious triathlete knows that the harder they work the fitter they become but also the more they are likely to encounter ailments that destroy their fitness. The key is finding the balance.

Overwork (too much, too fast, too soon) is still the main culprit and adherence to the basic principles of training, while closely monitoring signals from your body, can greatly assist in preventing problems.

heat and cold

Awareness of environmental conditions when training and competing is extremely relevant to the triathlon. The immensely popular Hawaiian Ironman is a good example of an endurance event held under extreme conditions. History has proven that care not only has to be taken during long distance events but shorter races as well. At the World Standard Distance Championships held in Florida in 1990, the high temperature combined with high humidity produced a significant casualty rate resulting in 13 hospital admissions for severe heat exhaustion with many other athletes requiring intravenous resuscitation in the medical tent following the race.

During exercise the conversion of chemical energy stored in ATP into mechanical energy is extremely inefficient with 70 percent of the total energy being lost in heat production during this conversion. This would raise the body temperature quickly above the comfort zone of 35-40 degrees Celsius, if the body could not use its built-in defence mechanism.

Heat is transferred away from the working muscle to the skin, either directly or through blood circulation. This process is called conduction. Air which circulates around the skin will then remove this heat, a process called convection. Heat will also radiate directly from the skin towards cooler objects close by.

Another method of heat loss is where sweat, produced by the sweat glands in the skin, is evaporated by the surface heat. It is the process of evaporation which dissipates the heat rather than sweating itself. This principle is important when competing or training in high humidity as in highly humidified air the process of evaporation is less effective. The two main factors which decide the effectiveness of heat control are the intensity of exercise and environmental conditions.

The environmental conditions relate to: the air temperature, wind speed, humidity and sun exposure. These will be discussed next.

exercise intensity

When exercising at high intensity the body has to decide between sending blood to the working muscle to supply oxygen or to the skin to help with heat dissipation. In this situation the body will favour an increased blood flow to the working muscle, thereby jeopardising the transfer process of the heat produced within the muscle to the skin.

air temperature

The lower the air temperature the easier heat is lost from the skin by convection. In rest the body's skin temperature is approximately 33 degrees Celsius. If exercising in temperatures greater than that, heat cannot be lost by convection because the air temperature is higher than that of the body surface. In this case the process will be reversed and the skin will heat up. In these conditions the athlete will become more dependent on the sweating/evaporation mechanism.

wind speed

Wind exposes the skin to a continuous stream of unwarmed air, allowing for effective convection. Running with a tail wind will have the opposite effect, as here the conditions come closer to being windless, preventing effective convection. In contrast, significant wind speed is often developed by cyclists making the convection process more effective. Heat is often, therefore, less of a problem for cyclists than it is for runners.

humidity

Sweating will only lose heat effectively through the accompanying evaporation. Usually a percentage of sweat drops from the body without evaporating. The higher the humidity, the less effective is evaporation.

sun exposure

The body can absorb heat from the environment, in particular from the sun. The body temperature is cooler than that of the sun and thus will absorb radiant energy from the sun if there is no cloud cover.

measuring the risk

Usually the dry air temperature is accepted as a rough measure of risk for heat stress when training and racing. To be more accurate, especially, for example, when racing in extreme conditions, other factors like humidity, wind speed and sun exposure need to be taken into account.

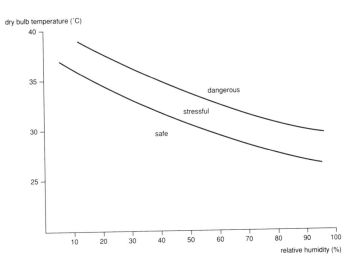

Fig. 1.

Using the simple diagram above (Fig. 1) the risk for heat stress can be assessed when competing in different environmental conditions of humidity and air temperature. The diagram shows that running and cycling at air temperatures of up to 25 degrees Celsius is relatively safe, even at a high humidity rate. Once the air temperature exceeds 27 degrees Celsius, increasing humidity greatly adds to the risk of heat stress.

dehydration and heat illness

Dehydration is a well known condition associated with endurance events, especially in a hot environment. When athletes lose more than 2-3 percent of their body weight through sweating, their performance will begin to drop. Thirst results when the body loses approximately 1 percent body weight. When 5 percent of the body weight is lost most athletes will show obvious signs of dehydration and heat illness. Dehydration levels of 7 percent or more are extremely dangerous.

Mark Allen showing the signs of competing in the heat after the end of the 1987 Hawaii Ironman

Many triathletes do not realise that water loss starts during the swim, through the skin and respiration. This is one of the reasons why fluid should be taken from an early stage on the bike before thirst sets in. Plenty of fluids need to be taken in the days before a triathlon to sufficiently hydrate the body. Alcohol has a dehydrating effect and should be avoided in the days before an event and in times of heavy training. A good guide to sufficient hydration is the frequent passing of clear urine.

Training and racing in hot weather can lead to chronic dehydration if no attention is paid to fluid intake and recovery (persistent thirst can indicate chronic dehydration). The best way to guard against chronic dehydration is to check your weight every morning. If there is a sudden decrease of more than 1 kg at times when no weight loss is expected, an attempt should be made to increase fluid intake.

Heat illness (heat stroke, heat exhaustion, heat syncope or hypothermia) usually occurs in combination with dehydration. Proper hydration is the main tool to prevent heat illness. The risk of heat illness is significantly increased by high temperatures, heat, humidity, bright sunlight and lack of wind, as the body's ability to lose heat depends on these factors. If the body's heat production is greater than the heat loss, an increase in body temperature and subsequent heat illness will be the result. Symptoms of heat illness usually occur when the central core temperature rises above 40 degrees Celsius.

Early symptoms of heat injury are:

- Excessive sweating or cessation of sweating
- Headaches
- Nausea and vomiting
- Dizziness
- Goose pimples

Further advanced symptoms are an impairment of consciousness, with initial confusion, disorientation and ultimately collapse. The early stages of heat illness can sometimes be overcome by slowing down and taking fluids frequently. More advanced heat illness requires medical attention. The diagnosis is confirmed by taking a rectal temperature. Treatment consists of the cooling of the athlete (using ice packs), along with hydration through intravenous fluids. If heat illness is not treated quickly and properly, serious complications can occur, such as kidney failure, an irregular heart beat, coma and death.

Research has shown that in well trained and acclimatised athletes the heat dissipating mechanism becomes more efficient. Proper conditioning and paying attention to hydration form the key to prevention.

Some athletes go better with heat than others due to the differences in heat generation and heat dissipation (the heat regulatory mechanism). Others will never be able to cope well with the heat despite taking every precaution. They are better concentrating on short distance and middle distance events held in moderate climatic conditions.

heat acclimatisation

It takes the body approximately 10 days to adjust to sudden increases in temperature and humidity.

Initially, on arrival, the heart rate will increase during exercise with an increase in core body temperature and a decrease in exercise tolerance time. The body will respond by increasing the plasma volume (retention of extra fluid by the circulation) and lowering the sodium chloride concentrations in the urine and sweat. The sweat rate will also increase. This will result in a lowering of the heart rate back to normal levels, a lowering of central body temperature and an increase in exercise tolerance time.

The risk of developing heat illness is greatest in the first five days of heat exposure. Of note is that although the increased sweat rate during heat acclimatisation will reduce the risk of heat illness, it will contribute to dehydration. Therefore, replacement of lost fluid becomes of paramount importance in preventing dehydration and subsequent heat illness **(see also Chapter 15, "Nutrition")**.

Following are some guidelines for heat acclimatisation:

-   Unfit individuals do not acclimatise as well as fit athletes. Untrained athletes should, therefore, not attempt to exercise at high intensity in the heat until an adequate level of fitness has been achieved.

-   For the fit athlete heat acclimatisation can be facilitated by exercising at an intensity greater than 50 percent VO_2 max. The total exercise/heat exposure time and the exercise intensity should be gradually increased during the first 10 days of hot weather training.

- Initially, do high intensity workouts in the cooler air temperature of early morning. Low intensity exercise can be performed during the hot midday hours.

- Monitor body weight daily.

- Wear loose fitting clothing that allows air to circulate through your body and expose as much skin to the air as possible to promote sweat evaporation. Light colours are better because they reflect rather than absorb sunlight. Sweat dampened clothing will not allow sweat to evaporate.

- Prevent dehydration. Weigh yourself before and after your workout. The weight difference is lost water. Thirty minutes before exercise, drink as much water and replacement fluid as is comfortable. A general rule of thumb for fluid replacement is to drink one full cup every 20 minutes during exercise. Afterwards, drink even if you are not thirsty. Alternate water with commercial sports drinks to help replace lost salt and potassium. Avoid drinks that contain caffeine or alcohol because they have a dehydrating effect.

- Be aware of the factors which reduce heat tolerance. They are: lack of sleep, infections and glycogen depletion as well as certain medications. There is some indication that anti-inflammatory tablets can increase the risk of heat illness.

- Reduce training intensity and duration when conditions are extremely harsh.

- Heat acclimatisation can be induced by wearing different layers of clothing in a cooler environment. This practice will make the transition to a hot training environment easier.

- The following groups have an increased risk for heat stroke: older athletes, overweight athletes, athletes who suffer from heart disease and athletes who have experienced heat injury before.

water intoxication

Water intoxication or sodium deficiency is now considered one of the more serious problems associated with endurance exercise. It is caused by excessive water intake over a prolonged period of time. This can cause the sodium level in the blood to drop to dangerously low levels, especially when so much sodium has been lost through sweating in hot weather. Nausea and cramps can be early signs. The more serious symptoms are disorientation, low blood pressure, fitting, coma, and even death.

The water intoxicated athlete is well hydrated and has a normal temperature, in contrast to the athlete with heat illness.

Water intoxication is less likely in middle distance events and rare in short distance triathlons. The risk can be reduced by heat training and the use of electrolyte drinks in addition to water and carbohydrates in events longer than four hours **(see also Chapter 15, "Nutrition")**.

cold exposure (hypothermia)

Cold exposure results when the body temperature drops below approximately 35°C and occurs when the rate of heat production from exercise cannot keep up with the rate of heat loss. Swimming in cold water is the most common cause of cold exposure in triathletes but cycling and running in cold weather can be responsible also, especially when those activities are preceded by a cold water swim.

Swimming in cold water is the most common cause of cold exposure in triathletes.

Shivering is an early warning sign and is initiated when body temperature falls slightly below normal. When the body temperature dips further the shivering will become less controlled and the athlete loses co-ordination and has difficulty speaking. Muscle cramps can also occur at this stage.

When the temperature drops below 35°C the athlete becomes lethargic and confused and the ability to shiver is lost. If there is no medical intervention unconsciousness and death may follow.

The diagnosis of cold exposure is confirmed by taking a rectal temperature. Treatment consists of warming and drying the athlete with dry clothes, blankets, towels and warm drinks. The more seriously affected athlete should not be encouraged to warm up through physical exercise as this can result in a serious irregularity in the heart beat and even cardiac arrest.

cramp

Cramp is characterised by sudden, involuntary, persistent cramping or spasms in the muscles. It occurs more quickly in an untrained muscle and, therefore, proper conditioning is paramount in the prevention of cramp.

Erin Baker stops suddenly to pick up a sun hat in the 1987 Hawaii Ironman causing her to cramp severely.

Cramp can also be caused by dehydration, excessive salt loss and possibly by trace element deficiencies of which calcium and magnesium are best known.

Salt depletion as a cause of cramp is not as common as generally thought but it can occur in long distance triathlon events held under extremely hot weather conditions. The triathlete who perspires heavily is more at risk. Acclimatisation before a hot weather race (ideally 10 days or more) will help to prevent excessive fluid and salt loss during the race. Athletes who have experienced cramp problems during hot weather conditions not caused by dehydration can try to add a little extra salt to their meals in the days leading up to the event. Salt tablets are not required.

Well-conditioned athletes who have persistent problems with cramp during training and/or racing need to seek medical advice to uncover underlying illness or trace element deficiencies. If all the tests are normal and the athlete does not respond to proper hydration, salt, calcium or magnesium supplements and even medication can be tried. Quininesulphate, for example, is known to be an effective and safe pill to help prevent cramp but should only be taken on the advice of a physician. Localised cramp is best treated with gentle stretching of the affected muscle.

low blood sugar

Cyclists call it "the bonk" (the sound the head makes when it hits the road), runners call it "hitting the wall". It is thought to be caused by a combination of depleted glycogen stores in the working muscle and an accompanying low blood sugar.

The symptoms are dizziness, general weakness, black spots in front of the eyes, possible headache, and excessive perspiration. It can occur during any form of endurance exercise lasting 90 minutes or longer.

It is usually caused by a combination of poor conditioning, not paying enough attention to carbohydrate intake, and poor pace judgement. Dehydration and heat illness can also contribute to "the bonk".

The problem is treated with an increase in carbohydrate foods and fluids, and a slowing down in pace until the athlete feels better. Flat Coke, in a diluted form, is an excellent medicine as the sugar and caffeine in Coke will give the struggling triathlete an instant lift.

It is preferable to prevent "hitting the wall", however, by sound conditioning, paying attention to carbohydrate and fluid intake **(see Chapter 15, "Nutrition")** and by proper pace judgement.

blisters

Blisters are most commonly encountered in running. Foot blisters are essentially burns produced by friction between the shoe and the skin. Blisters can be prevented by wearing good quality, well-fitting running shoes. Never wear new shoes in a race or in a long work out. Break the new shoes in by wearing them initially in shorter runs. Wet feet blister very quickly. If you wear socks, wear clean, snug fitting ones. According to research acrylic socks are most effective in preventing blistering. Thicker socks are better than thin socks and a double layer of socks is also effective in preventing blisters. Tape sensitive areas before training and/or racing. Using foot powder can also help prevent blisters.

The early stage of blistering is the development of a tender red area. When this happens tape the area until it has healed and wear different shoes in the meantime. Leave small blisters alone. They usually heal well if further friction is avoided and they can be taped during exercise.

Bigger blisters which cause pressure and pain require puncturing. Do this with a sterile needle and release the fluid by squeezing it gently. Do not remove the skin. It is important to keep the area clean to prevent infection; two or three days away from further friction (and running) is safest. Open blisters are best cleaned and dressed until healed because infection is a dreaded complication and can be prevented only by keeping the area clean. At the first sign of infection a physician needs to be consulted.

Chronic blisters, which do not respond to a change in running shoes, require attention from a physician or podiatrist. They can usually be treated by altering running form (through orthotics) or running technique.

stitch

Stitch is a common problem with triathletes. Stitch is a sharp pain near the bottom of the rib cage which can occur on either side or on both sides at the same time. It is thought to be caused by a spasm or cramp of the diaphragm (the large muscle which divides the chest from the abdomen), although the exact mechanism is not really known. Oxygen depth and faulty breathing are possible contributing factors. Recently it has also been thought that a muscle imbalance can contribute to this faulty breathing pattern.

Stitch mainly occurs during the run. Triathletes tend to be more prone to stitch than runners. It seems to have something to do with the folded up position they are in when they are cycling. Muscles and tendons attached to the lower rib cage will then be stretched acutely when straightening out going into the run, contributing to a superficial breathing pattern.

The possibility of stitch can be reduced by consciously attempting to breathe regularly and deeply using the abdominal muscles as support. This can be checked by putting a hand on the upper abdominal muscle while running. When stitch occurs during a run, lift both arms above your head while breathing in and lower them rhythmically while breathing out. Do this a few times and your stitch will most likely disappear.

If you have a muscle imbalance with weak abdominal muscles and tight back and groin muscles, then it is helpful to go on a stretching and strengthening programme. For this it is best to seek an opinion from a sports physician or physiotherapist.

colds and flu

Colds are caused by a virus affecting the lining in the nose and throat and sometimes the upper airways and sinuses, with the symptoms being a blocked nose, sore throat, headache and a cough.

The flu (influenza) is a systemic viral disease characterised by aches, pains and usually fever. Symptoms are usually more severe than those of a common cold and can last longer.

Colds and flu are usually contagious. The virus spreads through sneezing, coughing, shaking hands and touching contaminated articles. Once infected, the cold sufferer is susceptible to secondary complications like bronchitis, sinusitis, tonsillitis and ear infections that require medical attention.

There are a thousand and one remedies for the common cold and flu which really means there is no cure, so it has to run its natural course. Individuals vary in susceptibility. The average person usually suffers two or three episodes of colds or flu a year, but can experience more if exposed to a sufficient variety of viruses, or if bodily resistance is low. Athletes, although generally healthy individuals, are certainly not immune from colds and flu. Fatigue and exposure to excessive temperature changes can lower bodily resistance and here athletes need to take care.

Immunisation against the flu is generally available but will protect only against older flu viruses and not the latest ones. Salicylic acid (Aspirin and Disprin) and paracetamol help the aches and pains, and lower body temperature when there is a fever. Nasal sprays will unblock nostrils, inhalants help with blocked sinuses, and gargling with soluble Aspirin or Disprin may be helpful in alleviating a sore throat. All these measures can help to alleviate symptoms but will not shorten the illness.

Care has to be taken when taking over-the-counter remedies for flus and colds as some will contain banned substances, resulting in a positive result when drug tested.

During this time plenty of fluids need be taken - lemon and honey, diluted fruit drinks and plain water. Some people believe that megadoses of vitamin C (500-1000 gm/day) are not only a cure for colds and flu but will also prevent them if taken on a regular daily basis. This has yet to be confirmed by scientific evidence and, in fact, may cause adverse effects if taken over a long period.

The main thing most athletes are interested in when suffering from an illness is whether they can continue training. Serious complications can occur when exercising with a fever (a temperature higher than 37.4°C). When you suspect you have a fever, take your temperature (rectally) morning and night. A return to training is only safe when symptoms are improving and your temperature has been normal for at least three readings. Bedrest is still the preferred treatment for as long as the symptoms remain.

When recovering from a viral illness or when no fever is present, any training should be done with reduced intensity and duration, until symptoms have improved significantly. Listening to your body is crucial and often a few days' complete rest is safer and allows for a quicker overall recovery.

A medical opinion should be sought with prolonged symptoms (one week or more), or when there is a persistently high fever (above 39°C) despite taking Aspirin or Paracetamol.

Stomach flu (gastroenteritis) is also common amongst athletes. Symptoms include nausea, vomiting, stomach cramps, diarrhoea, aches and pains, and often a fever. Most stomach flus are caused by viruses but food poisoning should always be considered as a possibility. When symptoms persist for longer than 2-3 days other infections are usually responsible, and you might require medical attention. Symptoms associated with the gut can also be related to over-indulgence in alcohol, food allergies or nervousness, e.g. before a race.

The average stomach flu lasts approximately 24-48 hours and should be treated with bedrest and fluids only (water and/or diluted fruit juice) until the symptoms improve. Dairy products, fatty foods, alcohol, coffee and spicy foods can prolong the illness and are best avoided. If possible, it is advisable not to take medication to stop diarrhoea. This can prolong the illness as the virus will be contained in the gut longer.

runner's diarrhoea

"Runner's trots" is a common problem and can be resistant to therapy. Most runners have been caught out at one time and have learned through experience always to carry toilet paper on the run. For some, however, it is a more persistent problem returning at every training run or race, but it seldom occurs with cycling or swimming. The theory is that runner's diarrhoea is caused by lack of blood supply to the gut in favour of the working muscle, with additional bowel irritation through the mechanical mixing and bouncing of the bowel contents. Another cause of frequent bowel motions, which is easily correctable, is the increased dietary fibre intake which accompanies increased calorie intake necessary to sustain regular exercise.

Pre-race nerves can also be responsible for diarrhoea. Strategies to cope with this such as locating places of convenience near the start area and ensuring an empty bowel when the gun goes should be part of the overall race plan. Other measures which can be taken to reduce the chances of involuntary pitstops are a low residue (fibre) diet for 24-36 hours prior to competition together with a light early morning warm up and a drink of coffee or tea before the race to help stimulate a bowel motion before the event.

In some cases food allergies need to be excluded by a doctor or nutritionist. Using laxatives before a race or training, to empty the bowel, is not advised as it can contribute to dehydration. An effort should be made to defecate at a set time every day, e.g. after getting up in the morning. If nothing works then use a course for training which has toilets en route. Medication to stop the diarrhoea should only be used as a last resort and not on a regular basis. Lomotil and Immodium are both effective and safe. Codeine phosphate is effective, but on the list of banned substances. Nifedipine, which is a prescription drug, in a low dose, taken 30-60 minutes before exercise, will improve the blood supply to the gut and in the author's experience is very effective for runner's diarrhoea which does not respond to other measures or medication. However, side effects, e.g. headaches and dizziness, especially when taken in high doses, can defeat the purpose of taking this particular drug.

iron deficiency

Iron deficiency is now recognised as a common problem, for women more than men, among endurance athletes. Iron is required as a building stone by haemoglobin in the red cells, which carry the oxygen in the bloodstream to the working muscles. Iron deficiency, therefore, reduces work capacity by decreasing oxygen uptake.

Runners are known for their increased breakdown in red blood cells due to pounding on the roads. This pounding can cause micro-trauma to the lining of the bladder and gut also, with subsequent blood loss. Iron is also lost through sweating.

Women can lose a significant amount of iron during their menstruation which makes them more vulnerable to iron deficiency.

Iron is poorly absorbed in the gut so there is a fine balance between iron uptake and iron loss in the endurance athlete. Poor dietary habits can upset this balance easily, and be responsible for iron deficiency. Endurance athletes, therefore, need regular blood tests for haemoglobin, serum iron, iron saturation and serum ferritin levels, which are also called iron studies.

The serum ferritin level is the most sensitive measure for iron deficiency. A low ferritin level indicates low iron stores. If the serum ferritin falls below normal levels iron supplements and diet correction should be initiated. Symptoms usually occur when serum ferritin levels are significantly below normal. The symptoms are tiredness, a drop in performance, irritability, and sometimes itchiness. The nutritional aspects of iron deficiency are discussed in **Chapter 15, "Nutrition"**.

Iron medication should always be taken under medical supervision and it should be followed by regular blood tests. If a deficiency is persistent, a physician might have to exclude other illnesses through further tests. Ferrous sulphate (300 mg three times a day) is usually the supplement recommended unless it produces side effects such as nausea, constipation and diarrhoea. In this case, another iron preparation might be tried. Iron supplements will colour the stools black.

Iron is better absorbed when taken with meals and Vitamin C. Coffee and tea reduce the absorption of iron in the gut and should preferably be avoided when you are iron deficient.

injuries

Surveys done on triathletes show that the majority of injuries are running related. This is no surprise as the stress on the legs caused by pounding on the roads is considerable, and most injuries, therefore, affect the lower leg and foot.

Common cycling related injuries, except for those sustained in crashes, are located in the knee, lower back and neck. The swimmer's shoulder is one of the few injuries related to swimming.

It has been shown that more than half of all exercise injuries are caused by errors in training (too much, too fast, too soon). High mileage and intensity without allowing for suitable recovery and a sudden increase in training volume are the main culprits. Other causes are:

- Errors in technique: toe running, for example, can lead to many ailments in the lower leg.
- Faulty equipment: e.g. worn shoes, oversized bike.
- Inflexibility of muscles: the main cause of swimmer's shoulder. It also plays a role in many running injuries.
- Running surface: concrete and asphalt are hard on the legs.
- Structural abnormalities: flat feet, high arched feet, bow legs and knock knees can all contribute to running and cycling injuries.

Injuries always need to be distinguished from the normal aches and pains which come with training. These usually come and go, and are not severe enough to interfere with training. Usually they appear early during the training session and improve as the training progresses.

Alternatively, they can crop up at the end of a hard session with a quick recovery on cessation of training.

The following is a summary of some of the injuries that are commonly suffered by triathletes.

swimming

Swimmer's shoulder is caused by friction between the tendons, which are part of the capsule (rotor cuff) surrounding the shoulder joint, and the bone on top of the shoulder when the arm is rotated. When this happens often enough (the arm rotates approximately 1500 times in a 3000 m freestyle workout) these tendons, and the surrounding tissues, will become irritated and inflamed with subsequent pain, especially during movement. Swimmer's shoulder is a good example of an "overuse" injury, where the repetitive movement is the main cause of the ailment. In running and cycling often other factors play a role, such as shoes or positioning on the bike.

Swimmers with a perfect technique can still develop shoulder pain. It has been found, however, that there is a direct relationship between inflexibility of the shoulder and shoulder pain. Those with poor flexibility have much more chance of developing shoulder problems than those with good flexibility. The use of hand paddles can also contribute to shoulder injury and should be avoided by swimmers with poor flexibility or swimmers who have suffered shoulder problems in the past. Sports physiotherapists with an interest in this area will be able to give you advice on the state of your flexibility as well as how to improve it.

When the symptoms are mild and do not interfere with training they will often respond to ice massage following a workout. The emphasis at this stage should be on improving flexibility through specific stretching exercises. Bilateral breathing will prevent either shoulder from becoming overloaded. Some swimmers wear an upper arm strap in the early stages of swimmer's shoulder to help alleviate the symptoms.

Shoulder pain often occurs at the onset of a swimming programme or when the training volume is suddenly increased but when the shoulder gets stronger the symptoms can sometimes improve spontaneously.

In persistent and severe cases, where training is interrupted and pain is present for the remainder of the day after training (and sometimes at night), professional help is needed in the form of physiotherapy, anti-inflammatory medication, acupuncture or, as a last resort, a cortisone injection.

cycling

The most common knee injuries for cyclists are chronic sprains and strains of the ligaments supporting the knee joint and injury to the back of the kneecap. These injuries are caused, usually, by pushing too hard in high gears, or excessive hill climbing when the rider is not properly conditioned. Improper placement of the feet on the pedals may also place excessive stress on the ligaments supporting the knee joints. Toes pointing too far out can cause injury and pain to the inside of the knees, and toes pointed too far in cause injury to the outside of the knee joints. A seat position which is too high or too low can also cause strain on the knees.

Prevention and treatment of many knee injuries in cycling involves the use of lighter gears and correct placement of the feet in the pedals through careful angulation of shoe cleats. Cyclists who have knee problems caused by the structure of their feet and lower legs (flat feet, over-pronating feet, knock knees, bow legs, etc.) can often benefit from the use of carefully prescribed orthotics.

Back pain is a frequently encountered complaint in triathletes and cyclists. Most cases can be helped by adjusting the seat position (usually upward and forward) and/or by adjusting handlebar reach **(see Chapter 11, "Cycling" on position on the bike)**. The more experienced cyclist knows that initial lower back pain often improves gradually with conditioning. Many triathletes with more persistent symptoms have found relief with the aero handlebars, where the back is well supported by the buttocks and the elbows.

Back pain which does not respond to conditioning and adjustments to position on the bike should be assessed medically prior to treatment. If there is back pain with radiating pain, numbness, or pins and needles in the buttocks or legs, this should be taken seriously; an urgent medical opinion should be sought.

A new condition following the introduction of the aerodynamic handlebars is the aeroneck. This is neck pain and stiffness caused by sitting for long periods with the shoulders hunched, the arms tucked underneath the upper body and subsequent hyperextension of the neck. This position puts tremendous strain on the joints and tissues supporting the lower part of the neck. Symptoms can be improved by placing the elbow pads wider apart but also by practising the aero position as much as possible during training to condition the muscle groups involved.

running

Running injuries are mostly located in the knee, leg, ankle and foot. These injuries can often be attributed to abnormalities of the foot and foot plant. They can be helped by proper footwear, possibly the use of orthotics, and by paying attention to technique.

iliotibial band syndrome

Iliotibial band syndrome, a common injury in runners and cyclists, is caused by friction between the iliotibial band (a fibrous band running from the thigh on the outside of the leg to just below the knee joint) and a bony prominence just above the knee joint. This friction can lead to irritation and inflammation of the tendon with subsequent pain and tenderness of the outside of the knee joint. The iliotibial band syndrome is often caused by excessive pronation of the foot which causes, in its turn, excessive rotational forces on the outside of the knee joint. Mild symptoms usually respond well to correction through improved shoes, getting orthotics made, and applying ice. More serious symptoms might require intensive physiotherapy treatment, or, as a last resort, cortisone injections or surgery.

shin splints

Shin splints manifest themselves through pain along the inside of the shin. The name shin splint is used for three different conditions affecting the lower leg, or combinations of the three conditions.

1) Tendonitis (inflammation) of the tendons attached to the inside of the shin bone, which control the upward movement of the foot. This can be caused by weakness of the muscles concerned and also by a faulty foot plant (especially over-pronation), and by toe running. This condition usually responds well to correction of over-pronation, and technique, but also to specific strengthening exercises for the affected muscle groups.

2) Compartment Syndrome affects the muscles just behind the shin bone. When the muscle becomes too big for its surrounding sheath, especially when it swells during exercise, blood supply to and from the muscle will be compromised and pain develops.

3) Stress fractures of the shin bone. This is a relatively common injury with runners and persistent localised pain on the inside of the shin bone is always likely to indicate a stress fracture. These do not always show up on an X-ray and a bone scan may be required to confirm the diagnosis.

A stress fracture is one of the few injuries which requires complete rest from running. Often, however, triathletes will still be able to swim and bike. It usually takes 6-8 weeks for a stress fracture to heal.

A faulty foot plant (over-pronation), poor footwear and poor technique (overstriding, toe running) can all be contributing factors in shin pain. When symptoms persist despite a reduction in training, attention to footwear and running techniques, medical advice should be sought.

achilles tendonitis

Achilles tendonitis is a painful irritation and inflammation of the achilles tendon which connects the calf muscle to the foot at the back of the heel. Hill running without proper conditioning, and running on uneven terrain can be contributing factors, as well as wearing shoes with inadequate heel support. Biochemical problems like bow legs, tight hamstrings and calf muscles, high arched feet, over-pronation and toe running can aggravate this problem.

Five times more men than women suffer from achilles tendonitis. Treatment in mild cases consists of careful stretching following a thorough warm up, especially before more strenuous workouts, together with paying attention to shoes and icing following workouts. Putting a heel lift in your running shoe may help relieve pressure on the tendon. If more severe symptoms develop which interfere with normal training, seek advice from a physician or podiatrist.

plantar fasciitis

Plantar fasciitis is one of the more common injuries to runners. The plantar fascii is a band of fibrous tissue that runs under the bottom of the foot from the heel bone to the toes. It supports the arch of the foot and prevents the foot from collapsing under the body's weight. This fibrous band can become inflamed, especially at the attachment to the heel bone, with subsequent pain and tenderness along the inside bottom of the heel.

Running on hard surfaces, training in shoes with inadequate cushioning, doing excessive sprinting or uphill running without proper conditioning, and toe running can all contribute to plantar fasciitis. It can be prevented, and mild symptoms treated, by paying attention to shoes, avoiding running on hard surfaces, and by avoiding racing flats.

Once more severe symptoms are established it can be a difficult condition to treat and medical advice needs to be sought. It usually responds slowly to physiotherapy and anti-inflammatory medication. Special taping techniques can relieve the symptoms significantly. Acupuncture can also be helpful as well as a cortisone injection, although the latter should be a last resort.

illegal performance enhancing drugs

It would be naive to believe that "doping" is not used in the triathlon. It is one of the toughest endurance sports, requiring a tremendous amount of discipline, time and dedication. Many serious athletes give up their jobs and sometimes even their families for the sport. As well as the glory of victory, the triathletes' livelihoods depend on their performances to earn prizemoney and sponsorship endorsements. It is not surprising then that triathletes, as any other high-performing athletes, look at ways of improving their performance by means beyond training and diet.

Many countries have developed drug testing programmes for all sports including the triathlon. Strict dope testing for major races together with additional random testing for elite triathletes is the only way to prevent the triathlon from suffering a similar fate to athletics and other major sports where drug taking is more common.

Performance enhancing "drugs" which apply to the triathlon are the stimulants, narcotics, anabolic steroids, peptide hormones and miscellaneous drugs.

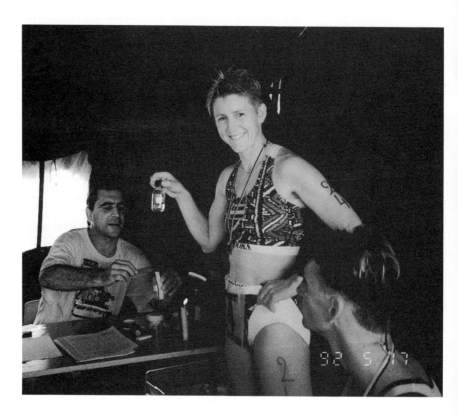

Drug testing prevents drug taking.

stimulants

(Nor) ephedrine, amphetamines and cocaine are examples of stimulants. They can be bought in small amounts in many countries, over the counter as remedies for such things as colds, flus and other minor ailments. Many slimming tablets contain compounds related to amphetamines. Amphetamines and cocaine, in particular, taken in higher doses, can induce mood elevation, a reduction in fatigue and an increased awareness. When taken during distance events it will improve subjective feelings (perceived exertion), rather than performance outcome. Stimulants can also produce addiction, hallucinations and anxiety, and can affect the heat regulatory mechanism. In hot, humid conditions they can prove fatal. Amphetamine abuse has been associated with numerous deaths in sport.

narcotics

Examples are codeine, morphine, pethidine and methadone. They mainly increase pain threshold and cause a feeling of euphoria. In theory they could be especially effective during long distance events. Serious side effects are the risk of physical and psychological dependence and respiratory depression. Except for codeine and selected compounds, they can also cause drowsiness which of course would defeat their purpose.

anabolic steroids

Anabolic steroids are substances related to the male hormone testosterone and among other things can accelerate muscle growth and repair. Popular examples are Dianabol, Durabolin, Winstrol (the Ben Johnson drug) and the Barcelona Wonder drug Clenbutarol (in Europe, an accepted medication for asthma!). They improve strength and are most effective when used during a period of heavy training.

The use of anabolic steroids can be stopped in the weeks leading up to an event without an immediate loss of the increased muscle strength. A doping test following the event will then be negative, which calls for the introduction of random testing at times when athletes are in serious training.

Anabolic steroids prescribed in a normal dose under medical supervision have few adverse effects. Athletes often use massive doses, however, on the assumption that if a little is good a lot is better. Under these circumstances women can develop male characteristics of which beard growth and lowering of the voice are the most obvious. They will also stop ovulating and menstruating. Given to children they can stunt growth. Men who abuse anabolic steroids assume female characteristics such as breasts, smaller testicles, and infertility. Some suffer from fluctuations in mood (anabolic psychosis, depression), low sex drive and water retention. The latter can cause swollen feet and legs. Abusers of anabolic steroids are at risk from heart disease including elevated blood pressure. Last, but not least, anabolic steroids can have a toxic effect on the liver, including the development of liver cancer. Anabolic steroids can either be taken per tablet (orally) or by injection (thereby bypassing the liver).

peptide hormones

In the last decade a new dimension has emerged with the abuse of growth hormone, a natural substance produced by the part of the brain called the pituitary gland. The boom in growth hormone abuse has resulted in pituitary glands (responsible for the production of the growth hormone) being taken from corpses and sold on the black market.

Its natural function is to stimulate growth until puberty and in medicine human growth hormone is used to treat children who are stunted in their growth because they do not have enough of the hormone. Excessive amounts given to children result in over-development of the skeleton and soft tissues (gigantism), with serious complications which often lead to early death. In athletes it is likely to cause a grotesque and excessive growth of the hands, feet and face. Additionally, growth hormones can cause diabetes as well as muscle and heart disease.

Little information is available on how, and how much, the use of growth hormone affects performance. The use of growth hormones is as yet difficult to detect.

Erythropoietin is one of the more effective (and dangerous!) drugs to improve endurance performance. It has made the practice of blood doping obsolete as it has a similar effect.

Erythropoietin is a hormone which is produced by the kidneys and which stimulates the production of red blood cells. Patients who suffer from kidney failure are given this drug to treat anaemia. Erythropoietin can now be made artificially and has therefore become more easily available. In healthy individuals it will boost the production of red blood cells and, therefore, the oxygen carrying capacity of the blood. It has been proven that blood doping and Erythropoietin provide a definite edge in endurance events. However, the cost can be high.

A serious side effect is excessive thickness of the blood which can cause strokes and heart attacks. In the literature, several deaths among cyclists who were taking Erythropoietin have been reported. Blood doping and the use of Erythropoietin are difficult to detect.

miscellaneous drugs

Miscellaneous drugs which are banned include corticosteroids (related to cortisone) and thyroid hormone. Little is known about the effects and use of thyroid hormone. Tests done on corticosteroids have not shown a significant improvement in performance.

legal performance enhancing drugs and methods

Athletes experiment continuously with substances claimed by an unscrupulous industry to have a significant effect on performance. More often than not those claims are unfounded, only backed up by unscientific, biased and anecdotal evidence. Co-enzyme Q, cytochromes, many forms and strengths of multi and single vitamins, bee products, pengamic acid (B12), ginseng, carnitine and several minerals are some of the long list of unsubstantiated boosters. Supplementation with vitamins, minerals and amino acids is only indicated where a deficiency is established or suspected. As training methods might have reached the limits of potential the athlete looks more and more for alternative ways of improving performance. Following are three examples of such methods which have received attention in scientific literature and which apply to endurance performance.

caffeine

Caffeine is probably the world's most popular stimulant drug. Besides being a stimulant caffeine also mobilises free fatty acids from the fat stores thereby stimulating fat metabolisim. Theoretically this can be beneficial in endurance events as this action will spare the carbohydrate stores. Caffeine taken in large doses (e.g. by pill or suppository) is banned by the I.T.U. The allowable limit for caffeine in the urine is 12 micrograms/ml. Below this you are safe. To put it in perspective, 6-12 cups of strong coffee are likely to put you in the danger zone.

Many Ironman participants have been saved during the later stages of a race by regular intake of Coke. Coke replaces fluid and energy, and the stimulating and carbohydrate sparing effects of the caffeine in Coke also play a role in the instant (although temporary) effects the athletes feel. However, this habit can lead to a positive test especially when the urine is already concentrated due to the effects of dehydration.

Some of the side effects of caffeine ingestion are a rapid heart beat, hand tremors, headaches, nervousness, nausea and diarrhoea.

Caffeine is also a diuretic. It stimulates urine production, adding to potential dehydration and thereby negating some of the positive effects of caffeine.

If you are not used to drinking coffee, try it out in training first. Tea also contains caffeine, appoximately half the amount as in coffee.

In general two cups of strong coffee 1-2 hours before a race could aid performance without breaking the rules.

bicarbonate loading
Much interest has focused on the use of bicarbonate loading on performance in recent years. There is some evidence that it can improve performance in middle distance running and swimming events. Bicarbonate neutralises the lowering in pH which occurs as a result of the accumulation of lactic acid in muscle and blood. A neutral pH is thought to assist the energy metabolism process which finds place within the muscle cell. Theoretically bicarbonate loading could also assist intense endurance performance although this has yet to be proven.

Performance effects of bicarbonate loading are dose related and a dose of 3 mg/kg body weight of (sodium) bicarbonate is the generally recommended dose, taken approximately 3 hours before the event. A common side effect is gastrointestinal upset with diarrhoea. This can be minimised by diluting the concentration of bicarbonate taken and spreading the intake out over a period of time, 2-4 hours before the race. The I.O.C. is currently considering banning this practice. Bicarbonate loading causes an alkalinisation (increase in pH) of the urine and is relatively easy to detect.

carbohydrate boosting
Another legal performance enhancing method is the use of high concentrations of carbohydrate solutions just before and during events. This goes one step further than carbohydrate loading, as the concentrations used are high (300 gm or more) and especially relate to the time in the hours before and during the event. Further studies are required regarding the effectiveness of these regimes.

glycerol loading
An interesting article appeared in *Medicine and Science in Sports and Exercise* (vol. 20, No. 4, 1990), the official journal of the American College of Sports Medicine. It describes a trial with glycerol, taken 2 hours 30 minutes before endurance exercise in a dose of 1 gm/kg body weight, combined with water (20 ml/kg body weight). The glycerol test was done on a cycle ergometer at moderate intensity for 90 minutes. The urine volume produced prior to exercise was reduced when glycerol was ingested, resulting in glycerol induced hyperhydration. During the exercise there was an elevated sweat rate and lower rectal temperature, indicating a possible effect on thermoregulation. Glycerol is a natural metabolite which is rapidly absorbed, has an osmotic effect (and thus has an ability to "hold" water) and is evenly distributed within the fluid compartments. Little is known

about this method of hyperhydration but theoretically this practice could have a performance enhancing effect in long distance events especially when weather conditions are hot, and a high amount of fluid loss is expected. In Ironman events smaller amounts of glycerol could be taken during the race, although this practice has not been officially tested.

It is clear that in unskilled hands serious complications can occur when taking drugs and it must be remembered that the medical profession has an obligation to discourage the use of performance-enhancing agents which are banned, and which are known to put athletes' health at risk. Because of this, athletes and coaches need to be educated on the potential hazards of drug abuse. The bottom line is, however, that besides being illegal, it is unethical for athletes to use performance-enhancing methods that are banned.

massage

Anyone who has experienced the luxury of a massage under skilled hands following a race or hard workout will agree that it helps recovery.

A good massage can break the vicious cycle of pain, muscle spasm and tightness by inducing relaxation. It improves circulation and, therefore, helps to remove waste products which have accumulated in the muscle during strenuous exercise.

Massage, and especially deep friction, can soften scar tissue and is, therefore, useful in rehabilitation following certain injuries. There is also the psychological benefit from the "laying on of hands", which can give the athlete confidence and encouragement. Massage should never be used as a substitute for warming up, however.

If time allows, the more serious triathlete will benefit from a weekly massage to keep the muscles supple during periods of hard training.

18

overtraining

Overtraining is one of the more common problems among serious triathletes. It is any short term or long term condition in which there is an imbalance between exercise and recovery, resulting in severe and prolonged fatigue.

Overtraining occurs either in athletes who train intensively for protracted periods, or who do a series of races in short succession, especially when continuing to train at high intensity between races.

causes of overtraining

For the working triathlete it is hard to find enough time to train in the three disciplines. Recovery time is often sacrificed. Lack of time for recovery (e.g. proper sleep) and relaxation will sooner or later catch up and result in injury and overtraining.

A long season, especially where the season is being extended by competing overseas, is another risk factor as is lack of positive reinforcement in the way of goals and expectations not being met. The free spirit of the triathlon, as it existed in the early 'eighties, has been taken away by the strict implementation of rules. The drafting debate, for example, has taken some of the fun out of competition and has added to the stress, therefore potentially contributing to the risk of overtraining.

In endurance athletes, chronic glycogen depletion can be an important contributing factor in overtraining during periods of heavy training. This can be prevented by proper dietary habits. Especially in hot climates, chronic dehydration can also contribute to the overtraining syndrome. The role of protein, minerals and trace elements in overtraining is unclear. The general stresses of life, e.g. relationships, work and study should not be underestimated in the role they can play in the cause and prevention of the overtraining syndrome. Causes of overtraining are summarised in Table 1.

Table 1.   **causes of the overtraining syndrome**

1. training and coaching errors

    a. Intense training for protracted periods
    b. Frequent racing
    c. Not enough recovery
    d. Length of season
    e. Lack of positive reinforcement
    f. Stringent rules
    g. High levels of competitive stress

2. nutritional deficiencies

    a. Carbohydrates (chronic glycogen depletion)
    b. Lack of protein
    c. Lack of minerals and trace elements
    d. Fluids (chronic dehydration)

3. psycho-social causes

    a. Relationships
    b. Study and work
    c. Other commitments

Overtraining needs to be distinguished from normal fatigue associated with training and other pathology, e.g. iron deficiency, anaemia, thyroid problems, viral illnesses (glandular fever) and infections. The difficulty is recognising, during periods of intense training, symptoms of overtraining. As long as there is not a dramatic drop in performance and the desire to train and compete is not lost, this is acceptable. However, during those times, careful monitoring of performance-related factors and overtraining symptoms is required.

prevention

It can be concluded that overtraining can be prevented through:

1. Proper training habits with variety and allowance for recovery.
2. Careful planning of the competitive season.
3. Optimal nutritional strategies.
4. Careful attention to study, work and relationships.

symptoms of overtraining

The single most important and first sign of overtraining is a drop in performance. This applies to performance in training (e.g. inability to finish a training session properly), time trials and racing. This is where a diary proves its worth. This will give ongoing feedback on training mileage, duration and frequency, also on weight fluctuations and changes in resting heart rate. Controlled time trials are an excellent monitor of fitness and overtraining.

The mistake many athletes make when their performance drops during times of hard training is to increase their efforts rather than reduce them. This attitude can then result in a fully blown overtraining syndrome. Most athletes do not accept that there is a limit to their individual performance capabilities and the first response to a plateauing of performance is to train harder rather than to train less.

Another common mistake is to increase training loads when feeling good and performing well following a period of hard training. You are better off easing back in training slightly and to aim at maintaining form rather than improving it.

Weight fluctuations and changes in resting heart rate are also significant indicators of overtraining. Another reliable guide is frequent illness and injury. Intense training lowers the resistance of the immune system, thereby exposing us to infections. Chronic overloading of the musculoskeletal system will increase the risk of overuse injuries and the accompanying fatigue will also affect technique, adding to the injury risk.

Chronic overtraining results in the occurrence of behavioural, emotional and physical symptoms. These are summarised in Table 2.

Table 2.   **common symptoms of overtraining.**

1. emotional and behavioural symptoms

  - Lack of enthusiasm and drive
  - Lack of motivation
  - Lethargy and excessive tiredness
  - Irritability, anxiety and depression
  - Inability to concentrate
  - Drop in academic performance
  - Problems sleeping
  - Loss of appetite
  - Loss of libido

2. physical changes

  - Reduced performance in training and racing
  - Weight fluctuations
  - Athlete looks unwell, drawn and dejected
  - Change in resting heart rate
  - Change in heart rate during and after exercise
  - Drop in blood pressure on standing (postural hypertension)
  - Persisting heavy leggedness
  - Persistent and progressive muscle soreness
  - Swelling of lymph glands
  - Gastrointestinal disturbances, e.g. diarrhoea and nausea

  - Increased susceptibility to infections, allergies, headaches and injuries
  - Poor healing of skin lesions
  - Amenorrhoea (loss of periods) in women
  - Increased fluid intake at night

chronic overtraining

Acute fatigue during or following exercise expresses itself either in breathlessness (from which recovery is quick) or fatigue of the muscular system (from which the recovery can take a few days).

Chronic fatigue is caused by a malfunction of the central nervous system. It is now thought that there are two types of chronic overtraining syndromes. The central nervous system can either go into overdrive or become severely depleted. Overdrive results in symptoms like irritability, sleeplessness, increase in resting heart rate, weight loss etc. When those symptoms are not recognised and the athlete keeps on training hard, the central nervous system becomes exhausted and depleted. Accompanying symptoms are excessive fatigue, excessive sleep, depression, lowering of resting heart rate and lethargy.

It is thought that the central nervous system depletion overtraining syndrome is often preceded by the central nervous system overdrive overtraining syndrome. If symptoms are recognised before the depletion phase sets in, a short period of rest can reverse the overtraining process. However, once the depletion stage has been reached, it can take 6-8 weeks or even longer of no, or little, training, for the symptoms to subside.

Table 3 highlights the differences between the two chronic overtraining syndromes.

Table 3.

overdrive central nervous system overtraining syndrome	depleted central nervous system overtraining syndrome
Reduced performance in training and racing	Reduced performance in training and racing
Increased heart rate at rest and during submaximal exercise	Decreased heart rate at rest and during submaximal exercise
Delayed recovery of heart rate after exercise	Rapid recovery of heart rate after exercise
Emotional instability	Phlegmatic behaviour/depression
Problems sleeping	Excessive sleeping
High blood pressure	Low blood pressure
Normal blood sugar response during exercise	Low blood sugar response during exercise

Severe forms of chronic overtraining can result in an illness known as Addison's Disease. The symptoms are progressive weight loss, depression, inability to maintain blood pressure when standing and severe physical incapacitation. Addison's Disease is caused by a failure of the adrenal glands to secrete adequate amounts of certain hormones, in particular cortisol. The adrenal gland, like other hormone producing glands, depends on the central nervous system, in particular on an area in the brain called the hypothalamus, for its activation. An exhausted hypothalamus can then result in general depletion of the hormone producing system. This fits in with symptoms of overtraining like depression, loss of appetite and loss of libido, which all depend ultimately on the function of the hypothalamus.

There are no reliable tests as yet to diagnose the overtraining syndrome. This means that personal, close and continued observation of the athlete by the coach provides the key rather than any specific scientific test. If there is little coach/ athlete contact, which is often the case in triathlons, triathletes have to be aware of the overtraining syndrome and learn to listen to their bodies.

19

duathlons and multi-sport

duathlons

The run, bike, run started in the early '80s, initially to accommodate triathletes who had problems with swimming. The official distances for the duathlon are the 10 km run, 60 km bike, 10 km run and the 5 km run, 30 km bike and 5 km run. However, many variations exist. In recent years the duathlon has become as popular as the triathlon in many countries. The time when triathletes dominated duathlons is over.

The duathlon has created its own breed of champions. Specific training is required if you want to be competitive in this cycling time trial sandwiched between two runs. During the first run the pace is often as fast as any straight out road run. The legs do not completely recover from this during the bike ride and the second run is, therefore, started when the specific running muscles are already significantly fatigued.

Special training is required to condition the muscles for this. Many duathletes, for example, use brick sessions. These are short run-bike-run repetitions either on the road or with the use of windload trainers and/or treadmills. This is where training specificity comes in. The same principles of periodisation and cyclic training apply to the duathlon as to the triathlon. Table 1 gives a sample programme for a competitive duathlete, training for a 10 km-60 km-10 km event, for the eight weeks leading up to the event.

Table 1.

	run	bike
monday	1 hour including repetitions	90 mins easy-steady
tuesday	45 mins steady	2 hrs including time trial up to 50 mins
wednesday	90 mins - 2 hrs in the hills	90 mins - 2 hrs
thursday	Bike - run repetitions either up hill or on the flat	
friday	REST DAY OR EASY JOG	
saturday	30 mins to 45 mins x 2 Run-bike-run in continuous fashion	90 mins - 2 hrs
sunday		3 - 4 hours

Comments:

-   This is a sample programme for a serious duathlete, based on five sessions per week per discipline.

-   The order of disciplines practised on different days should vary.

-   Saturday has a continuous run-bike-run session to mimic race conditions and distance.

-   Thursday will have run-bike-run repetitions. The length, frequency and intensity of repetitions can vary. The repetitions can either consist of hill repetitions (hard up, easy down) or flat repetitions, depending on the nature of the event for which you are training. The bike reps can also be done on the windload trainer, alternated by run reps. Examples of repetitions are 6 x 2 mins for each discipline or 3-4 x 4-5 mins per discipline. This can be done either continuously or with shorter or longer rest periods between each run-bike or bike-run.

Table 2. **sample programme for a recreational duathlete who trains for a 5 km-30 km-5 km event.**

	run	bike
monday	20-30 mins	
tuesday		30 mins - 60 mins
wednesday	1 hour	
thursday		60 - 90 mins
friday	REST DAY	
saturday	20 mins	45 mins
	15 mins Run-bike-run in continuous fashion	
sunday	FAMILY DAY OR FREE DAY	

Comments:

- This programme is based on three sessions per discipline per week, including one transition session.

- The pace is easy or steady depending on the fitness.

- In the early phase of this programme duration needs to be increased before pace is increased.

- Race pace should not exceed training pace.

multi-sport events

Multi-sport events incorporate different disciplines compared with the conventional swim, bike, run. In cooler climates, or in winter, the swim can be replaced, for example, by a canoe or ice skating event. The choice often depends on the available natural terrain. In the Southern Hemisphere canoeing triathlons have become very popular as the rivers and lakes lend themselves to this activity. The world famous New Zealand Coast to Coast race, a 238 km race from the West Coast to the East Coast of the South Island, incorporates cycling, mountain running and white water canoeing. This is a good example of a triathlon which makes excellent use of natural terrain, much of which is some of the most beautiful in the world.

Multi-sports often require a completely different dress code.

In countries like the Netherlands the winter triathlon consists of a run, bike, speed skate, and in more mountainous countries snow shoeing and cross country skiing are often included. Similar training principles apply here as to any other multi-sport endurance events, in the sense that it is specificity which counts. You will need to train in a particular discipline if you want to feel comfortable racing and especially if you want to be competitive. Specialised equipment is often required. For many triathletes, the three disciplines, along with equipment and training concerns, are enough to cope with. Therefore, they prefer to spend the off season on single discipline training or duathlons.

Recent years has seen the emergence of multi-stage events run over many days, again often incorporating the challenge of natural terrain. Those races can be done either as a team or as an individual. Events including mountain biking have also become popular in many countries. All those events have added to the status of the sport of triathlon and there has been a tremendous increase in awareness and participation in multi-sport events. The variety and challenge offered by these events have given a completely new dimension to the triathlon and opened the sport to much wider participation.

20

masters in triathlon

effects of ageing on exercise

Age group competition has taken off in the last decade and the triathlon has been in the forefront of this development. Currently the age groupers form the backbone of our sport. In most races not more than 10 percent of the field consists of pro athletes, the rest are made up of fiercely competitive age groupers and triathletes who take part just to finish, for fun, health and fitness.

This chapter will concentrate on the 40-plus age group. The two issues for this group are how increasing age affects performance, and also to what extent regular exercise can minimise the ageing of different bodily functions.

Scientists still argue whether we lose speed before endurance or endurance before speed when getting older. It is certainly true that in endurance sports older athletes can still be very competitive compared with the more explosive, speed sports.

Researchers have found that there is little change in performance characteristics until the early 30s with the peak usually in the late 20s for endurance sports, after which there is a gradual decline in performance of approximately 6-10 percent per decade. This is a general statement and there are many anecdotal exceptions which confirm this rule. The main reason many competitive athletes give up in their late 20s seems to be more related to mental aspects, e.g. motivation, than physical deterioration.

The emergence of the age group system will hopefully keep more athletes in the sport, as it obviously brings new incentives every five years. Table 1 summarises the effects of ageing on bodily functions related to endurance exercise.

Table 1.   **effects of ageing on bodily functions related to endurance exercise.**

1. Lowering of VO_2 max.

2. Shift of lactate turn point to a lower speed or exercise intensity (shift to the left).

3. Lowering of heart minute volume thus lowering oxygen carrying capacity of the blood and therefore endurance.

4. Lowering of maximal heart rate.

5. Reduction in elasticity of muscles and connective tissues resulting in a reduction in strength and increased risk of injury.

6. Reduction in muscle contractility resulting in reduced strength and power.

7. Reduction of tolerance to extreme temperatures resulting in increased risk of heat illness and cold exposure.

8. A lowering of the basic metabolic rate, due to the reduction of the total amount of mitochondria in the muscle cell, affecting aerobic metabolism.

9. Reduction of the vital capacity of the lungs.

10. Reduction of total bone mass.

For the experienced competitive triathlete Table 1 is grim reading. It must be said, however, that for the novice older triathlete, who has no or little background in exercise, all the mentioned bodily functions improve for the first few years, before declining after reaching peak level.

effects of exercise on ageing

The effects of inactivity on our bodily functions are very similar to the effects of ageing. Regular exercise, therefore, will have a beneficial effect and keep the changes which come with ageing to a minimum.

Health aspects of the triathlon become more important with age. It is well accepted that endurance exercise contributes to a longer and healthier life. Because a varied exercise programme is easier to complete, what better excuse do you need to become involved in the triathlon. Swim one day, bike the next (on your home trainer if you wish) and run the third, all between 20 and 30 minutes; repeat the sequence and somewhere in between have one rest day and you have the ideal weekly recipe to (almost) eternal life. This is especially true when attention is also being paid to proper nutrition and the stresses of life.

But it is not always that easy, as many 40-plus triathletes want to compete as much and as hard as the younger ones. Perhaps they do not look so much for improvement but refinement in their performance, or at least, to maintain their speed and endurance for as long as possible.

Many 40-plus triathletes want to compete as much and as hard as the younger ones.

When looking at performance in relation to age, it is crucial not only to look at chronological age, but also at the training age. The "prognosis" for a 40-year-old who is a novice at the sport is very different from that for the 40-year-old veteran triathlete who has competed for many years at a high level. The latter is unlikely to show any real improvement in performance and is wise to aim at a strategy which minimises the effects of ageing on performance. The novice age grouper can look forward to an approximate six-year spell of continuous performance improvement in the three disciplines if they follow appropriate training programmes. Although the veteran master athlete in the end will still beat the novice most of the time, it is likely that the novice has more fun in the process.

The problem novice triathletes have is often with the swimming segment of a triathlon. It is relatively easy to conquer the skills of jogging and cycling, but the technically more demanding discipline of swimming can present a real hurdle as it is harder to learn new skills in later life. Attracting masters to the sport can be enhanced by having special training sessions for masters, as well as organising special events, including duathlon options for the non swimmers and events using a swimming pool rather than the open water.

Except for a slow reduction in performance over time, there are two main problems facing the older triathlete. The first is an increased risk of injury because of the reduced elasticity of muscles and tendons and secondly there is generally a slower recovery rate from intense training and racing.

In general, older athletes have a lower training capacity so the principle of doing a little less rather than a little more applies, especially to the more experienced and more competitive master triathlete. This includes being moderate in setting training programmes, setting realistic goals and competing less frequently. The use of heart rate monitors can assist the older athlete in monitoring training intensity.

Following are some tips on training for the older triathlete.

- Avoid high impact exercises, e.g. intense plyometrics or fast downhill running.
- Space harder sessions properly to allow for sufficient recovery time.
- Race less. A rough guide is 4-6 short distance races per season or 2-3 middle distance races. Not more than one Ironman race is recommended.
- Pay attention to muscle flexibility and balance, as muscle imbalances often become more pronounced with time.
- Pay extra attention to training and racing in extreme temperatures.
- Watch the balance of life, unless you are single and have no dependants.

21

women in triathlon

There are many unanswered questions associated with women's involvement in the sport.

The fact that there are not large numbers of women participating in sport, and especially in triathlon, is a result of many factors. Many of these can be traced to social pressures which have not afforded women the same opportunities or encouragement to compete or take part as men. There is also additional social conditioning, which, evolving for centuries, has dictated the roles of men and women in society.

There is a great depth of untapped triathlon talent waiting to be uncovered amongst female competitors around the world. In years to come there will be a great improvement in women's achievements in endurance athletics, especially as more females enter such events.

In Western society, sport is one of the last frontiers where man can assert his superior strength. Women have come a long way since the ancient Olympics in Greece where they were punished with the death penalty for simply watching the competition. But the prevailing attitude in the male-dominated sports scene is still, unfortunately, that sports participation by women is contrary to femininity.

Men often feel threatened when women show superiority in "their" domain and will subsequently become critical about women's ambitions. A lot of the time the woman is competing alongside the male athlete and on his terms, which means that she is poorly coached, inadequately supported and will only attract public attention if she is attractive. This attitude of the male-dominated sports world (and the triathlon is no exception) has prevented many women from entering competitive sports.

women differ from men

Physically and psychologically women are different from men. Physical differences are hormonally determined. Women have less muscle mass (23 percent of a woman's body is muscle compared with 40 percent for a man) and more fat. This means that they will never be able to compete equally with men. But, some of the disadvantages are compensated for by the fact that women's muscle characteristics are more suitable for endurance exercise compared with men's muscles which are generally more suited to explosive functions. This, with their lighter weight, explains why women can excel more in endurance exercise requiring stamina and efficiency of movement rather than in explosive sports requiring power and speed.

Another disadvantage for women is that in general they have fewer red blood cells and a lower haemoglobin concentration in their blood, resulting in lower oxygen-carrying capacity then men.

It is a common misconception that sports participation has a masculinising effect on female performers. The body form of females and males is largely the result of genetic design. Research has shown that heavy training will not alter the female athlete's shape to the extent that occurs when males train. Some of the top women athletes who have a predominance of male physical characteristics (and excel for that reason) have not gained these through training but have inherited them.

In the social environment as it is now, women athletes have to be independent and hard-headed to succeed. Social pressures have no doubt contributed to the superior psychological characteristics which the female competitors have over their male counterparts. Naturally some of those characteristics are also inherited.

In general, women are tougher, more constant, more enduring, more independent, more patient, more level-headed and calm, during training and racing than their male counterparts. They also tolerate pain and exertion to a greater degree. It is obvious that these characteristics make women suitable for endurance exercise.

Although men are more explosive, inconsistent and less enduring, it has to be made clear that this is a generalisation comparing groups of women athletes with groups of men, and obviously some male athletes have also superior psychological characteristics.

menstruation

One area involving women which is continually avoided but which probably concerns them most, is the effect their menstrual cycle has on their athletics pursuits.

In general, you can train and race while you have your period. If you are lucky you will find your period will seldom occur on race days. This is due to the effects your physical and mental build-up to the race has on your hormonal system. It will often come a few days following the event or even a month later. Some of the elite triathletes stop having their menstruation altogether during heavy training schedules.

This is called athletic amenorrhoea when the absence of periods is at least six months. Athletic amenorrhoea can have long term effects on the body if not monitored and/or treated. The main problem associated with this condition relates to bone mass. It has been found that amenorrhoeic athletes are prone to low bone density (brittle bones) which can lead to stress fractures during a women's sporting career and to osteoporosis in later life. Peak bone mass is reached at age 30-35, yet many female athletes have decreasing bone density at this particular time. Although the problem can be partly reversed when periods do reappear, it is not known and doubtful if it is possible to catch up and reach normal peak bone mass. All this means that women should be concerned when menstruation ceases (for no obvious reason) and it is important to consult a sports medicine physician if six periods are missed or the very first period has not occurred by age 15-16.

Contributing factors to this condition include hormonal changes, low body fat levels and psychological stress. The hormonal changes are in part induced by the rigorous training regimes many women undertake.

Diet can play a role in the onset of athletic amenorrhoea. Poor nutrition in general has been implicated and more specifically low energy, fat and protein intakes, vegetarian diets (especially avoidance of red meat) and excessive intakes of fibre have been associated with amenorrhoea.

Although it may be tempting to ignore the cessation of periods or even be tempted to feel pleased with it, it is important that you seek a medical opinion and that appropriate investigation and management is initiated.

Periods usually return spontaneously when training diminishes. Most women, however, especially those training at a more social level, will continue to have their periods as normal. Dealing with this in the triathlon is no different from what you have probably dealt with for many years.

If your period does happen to fall on a race day this will affect your confidence mainly. There is no reason not to compete unless your period is heavy. Do not feel embarrassed. After all, it happens to half the population.

There is little evidence that performance of women as a group is seriously affected by the menstrual cycle. Women in all stages of their monthly cycle have won Olympic gold medals. If you are serious about competing and do feel that having a period during a race will affect your performance negatively, you can easily postpone your period by medication prescribed by your doctor. Make sure though that you have tried this before the race.

bras and breasts

The popular concept that most elite athletes are flat chested is entirely false. Some most certainly are, but there are plenty with good-sized chests and there are many good sports bras available that will give you the support you require, especially for running.

If you find you require plenty of support there is no reason why you cannot wear a bra under your swimsuit. Often there are few changing facilities at transition areas so have your bra on from the start. It will dry easily during the bike and give you the support needed during the run. Do not be embarrassed by having to wear a bra under your running singlet or during the swim. To compete to your optimum you must be comfortable.

pregnancy

It has been shown that pregnant women who exercise regularly have in general a healthy pregnancy and an easier and shorter labour. Studies have shown that they often require less or no pain killers during childbirth and that they are more in control of events.

It appears that a good maximum oxygen uptake, which is acquired through general fitness training, is helpful in coping with the workload of labour. In general there is no evidence that exercise has negative effects on the fetus. However, most research is done on short term sub-maximal exercise and not much data is available on high intensity exercise of long duration, which triathlons are all about.

Theoretically, blood could be shunted away from the placenta to the working muscles, which over time could deprive the baby of the necessary oxygen and nutrients to grow. Dehydration, a relatively common occurrence during endurance exercise, could compound this problem.

The first three months is usually the most vulnerable time during pregnancy because of the risk of miscarriage. Jarring exercises should be avoided and for women who have had a miscarriage before, during the first three months it is safer to avoid jogging.

Later in pregnancy there are mechanical reasons why triathlon events become less attractive. Running often becomes plain uncomfortable and bikes need to be adjusted.

Swimming is by far the best, most all-round exercise for pregnant women. Thirty to 45 minutes, up to 3-5 times a week, under controlled conditions and most of it at sub-maximal intensity, is the most effective, safe and enjoyable way to childbirth. Combined with regular back exercises, this would be the ideal prescription for activity during pregnancy.

In summary, it is my advice for the pregnant athlete to temporarily put her triathlon aspirations on hold and concentrate on general health and fitness, with an emphasis on non-weight-bearing exercise, to prepare for the ultimate event, which is childbirth.

contraception

Women who exercise use the same type of contraceptive methods as those who do not. Some of these methods can have implications for the more serious exercising female although the available information is sparse. The barrier and chemical method of contraception (condoms, diaphragm and spermicidal agents) have no effect on exercise capacity and performance. IUDs (intra-uterine device) on the other hand can cause pelvic infection and abnormal bleeding. This can interfere with performance and enjoyment. Increased blood loss can lower the haemoglobin concentration in the blood and contribute to iron deficiency.

The oral contraception pill causes physiological changes. Few studies have been done on how the pill affects exercise capacity although there is a possibility that the pill may actually be advantageous as it can increase blood volume and heart function to some degree. There is no evidence of any extra risk involved from exercising when on the pill.

Possible side effects of the pill are nausea, weight gain, headaches, depression and a general feeling of being unwell. Obviously, these symptoms can interfere with enjoyment and performance, and a change to a different pill or another contraceptive method is appropriate.

Long-acting progesterone injections can frequently cause irregular bleeding and fluid retention, and are not advisable for women involved in strenuous exercise programmes.

encouraging women to take part

Ninety five percent of all women could take part comfortably in a short distance triathlon. They would, of course, need to put in a certain amount of training.

Swimming, for both sexes, is the major hurdle. This can be overcome by joining a swimming group and learning the basics properly. Another way to get involved in the sport is to form a team and participate in a triathlon relay. Most triathlons nowadays have a relay race incorporated in the event. This can be one of the most enjoyable ways of attacking the sport, and also one of the most overlooked.

If you are a weak swimmer then team up with someone strong in that discipline. With a three-person team you only have to complete one of the disciplines. Having competed in a couple of these events, you will perhaps have developed the confidence to look at tackling the full event.

The sport has grown so much in recent years that you will not have to look far to find a small event - maybe a 200 m swim, 15 km cycle and 5 km run. And, if you find competing alongside men intimidating so early in your career, there are now events being organised just for women. Women's triathlons have proven to be very successful, attracting a wide range of women, many of whom would have been too intimidated to mix it with the men.

Erin Baker, the dominant figure in triathlons in the last decade.

Women who work and have a family often become very time efficient and inventive when it comes to finding time to train. Sharing training groups with other women in similar positions, by which the babysitting and training is shared, is a very effective way to train. This, of course, becomes more difficult when training for an Ironman event but it does work for shorter races. Alternatively, with an early morning swim (husband gets the kids ready for school) followed by either running or cycling to and from work, you can use your normal travel time as part of your training. If you cannot train before work then utilise your lunch hour. It is normally a time when you just sit and talk or eat. The therapeutic value of a lunchtime workout is immense.

By rising one hour earlier in the morning you can overcome the need to train in the evening. Time for training should be looked at positively.

barriers

As well as having many strong points, women also have their perceived weaknesses. But, these can be overcome.

For those wanting to compete in a social event, often not enough training is done. If you only wish to finish a race then that is fine, but if you are by nature competitive, and wish to improve, then you must overcome the notion that women are not as good as men, not as strong, and, therefore, cannot do the same training. This is false. Elite triathletes of both sexes will do about the same amount of training.

In women's competition there is an enormous gap between the top athletes and the rest, whereas with men there always seems to be a new star coming through to keep the pressure on. No one can afford to rest on their laurels. If a man has an off-day he will be beaten. An elite woman can also have such a day but still win because there are not the women athletes around to challenge and hustle. Many women are reluctant to take that step from being a sub-elite to an elite athlete because it takes hours of extra toil and they are not prepared to make the commitment compared with men. While women's psychological powers may be stronger they are less inclined toward the discipline required to train, and to train on an ordered basis.

22

children in triathlon

With all the publicity the triathlon has been exposed to, more and more young people are being attracted to the sport. The result is the creation of a special breed of triathletes with unique psychological and physical characteristics suited to multi-disciplinary events. The physical demand that the triathlon imposes means the average child will have difficulties coping with the distances and effort required, and it is not surprising that most triathlons carry a lower age limit of 16. As a consequence of the phenomenal growth of the sport in recent years, we have seen the introduction of triathlons for children which are raced over much shorter distances than the classic short distance event 1.5 km swim, 40 km cycle and 10 km run. Common distances are 100-500 m swim, 2-20 km bike, 1-5 km run.

The triathlon is a unique sport in that it encompasses all health-related fitness variables and, therefore, can be used as a prime example of health-related fitness. It is an endurance activity which uses nearly all the muscles of the body so cardio-respiratory endurance is developed as well as strength and endurance in the major muscle groups. Apart from the health-related quality of the triathlon it is fun and an achievable activity for most children. All children can run, most can swim and ride a bike.

Competing is the important aspect, not the quality of equipment.

There are no complicated skills involved as in team sports. Failure to succeed in skill-related activities such as soccer, basketball, gridiron, baseball, rugby, and netball may discourage a child from exercise. It may create the negative perception that physical activity is limited to elite athletes. But, to finish a triathlon gives tremendous satisfaction and contributes to psychological development and self-confidence. Children are often very competitive and although it is not necessary to compete in races to achieve the benefits of regular aerobic exercise, the motivation provided by the challenge of organised races may be vital in maintaining the child's interest in fitness.

children are different

Although triathlons are safe for children to participate in, we have to give special consideration to the unique features of the growing child. There are no differences in strength, body size and mass between girls and boys until the physical changes begin to appear at the onset of puberty. This means that boys and girls under the age of 12 can compete against each other.

It is stressed, however, that particularly in this younger age group, the emphasis should be on participation rather than competition. Maturity is not always directly related to age. Late-maturing children have an obvious disadvantage in sport and late, slow-maturing children come in all sizes. They are not necessarily small in stature. Some are large and obese, with immature skeletal strength and limited muscle mass. There are also tall, non-obese children, who are going to be delayed maturers because of their prolonged growth. The triathlon, which is very much an individual event, can give these children confidence, enjoyment and satisfaction without the extra risks they are exposed to when they play contact sports. Children who mature early are easily recognised by their sporting success. Care must be taken that the child's results are not over-estimated as the successes are due to the fact that the child is heavier, stronger and faster than other children of the same age group. The child's future career depends on the attitude of the parents/coach towards success. The triathlon gives the early maturer the opportunity to participate and compete with individuals of similar maturity.

Children have different anaerobic and aerobic capacities from adults. They have poor tolerance for anaerobic activity and a high level of aerobic power. The triathlon is an aerobic event. This means that, in general, children cope well with submaximal exercise, especially if the level of skill involved is not too high. But children do not tolerate environmental temperature changes as well as adults. Firstly, they have a higher body surface area to mass ratio which creates greater exposure to environmental temperature changes. Secondly, they have greater heat generation for a given activity and thirdly, children perspire less. Because of this, special precautions must be taken in triathlons for children to protect the participants from the effects of extreme environmental temperatures.

Because of their shorter extremities (resulting in a short stride, stroke) and immature technique, children have to work harder and expend more energy to cover the same ground, and so, have a lower motor efficiency than adults.

Compared with adults, children perceive exercise automatically within the limits of comfort. They have an intuitive ability to listen to their own bodies' demands. Children will only pass their perception of their physical limitations because of outside pressure, e.g. parents or coach.

A common observation is that children recover from strenuous exercise more quickly than adults. The reason for that is not clear, although some of it can probably be attributed to their reluctance to push themselves beyond their physical limitations.

triathlon training for children

Table 1 is an example of a training programme for a 12-17 year old preparing for a first-time triathlon and with the main aim to finish the event. The majority of children will fall into this category. Intense competition is not advocated for every child.

Table 2 shows a training programme for the more competitive child triathlete aged 15-17 years. For 6-12 year olds structured training programmes are not recommended. Children of that age are usually exposed naturally and playfully to the three disciplines during and after school. All of the sessions for the first programme need to be done at a comfortable aerobic pace. Competitive swimmers in the 12-16 year age group can be safely exposed to high intensity swim training. Interval training for running and cycling can be introduced for the 15-17 year age group. But, it is stressed that training schedules for the more competitive triathletes should be individualised.

Weight training has no place in a triathlon training programme for children but strength training, using natural resistance (hills for running and cycling, swimming with arms only), is safe. Combined sessions of the different disciplines will prepare the child to cope with the transitions and as most of the training is done at a comfortable aerobic pace, few risks are involved. The children will soon learn to pace themselves through training sessions.

It is advisable to do most of the swim training in a pool, but the child should have been exposed to the experience of open water swimming at least once before entering a race. This should always be done under supervision and only if the water temperature is at least 16°C. For safety reasons the use of a helmet during cycling training is strongly recommended and to prevent running-related injuries, the child should have proper footwear. Children should be encouraged to run as much as possible on natural surfaces like grass, forest tracks and the beach at low tide.

Swimming in a pool is a great idea.

Table 1.	training schedule for a triathlete, age 12-17, enabling them to finish a short event comfortably		
	swim	bike	run
monday	30 mins		
tuesday		30-45 mins	
wednesday			30 mins
thursday	30 mins		
friday		rest day	
saturday	30 mins	30 mins	15-30 mins
sunday		45 mins-1 hr or	30-45 mins

Note:
- Spend any extra available time on your weak discipline.
- Try and get some basic tuition and coaching in training and technique.
- The Saturday session is done in a continuous way to familiarise the body with the transition effect.

Table 2.	training schedule for a competitive triathlete, age 15-17		
	swim	bike	run
monday	45 mins-1 hr	1 hr	
tuesday	45 mins-1 hr		45 mins-1 hr
wednesday		1 hr 30 mins-2 hrs	
thursday	45 mins-1 hr		45 mins-1 hr
friday		rest day	
saturday	30 mins	45 mins	30 mins
sunday		1 hr 30 mins-2 hrs or	1 hr

Note:
- Basic conditioning in 3 disciplines is required before a programme like this can be attempted.
- Tuition on training methods and technique is essential for the competitive child triathlete.
- This programme is based on 3-4 sessions a week per discipline, or 9-12 altogether.

This will give an improvement in performance with little risk of overuse injuries and overtraining.

triathlon competition for children - tips for organisers

swim

For 8-12 year olds, have the swim in a pool, preferably around the perimeter so that the wall is kept close by. To thin out the congestion, consider having the swim last or alternatively start the race in heats. Restrict the distance to 25-100 metres. The water temperature should be a minimum of 16°C for this age group.

The 12-17 year olds can swim in open water. Make sure there are plenty of rescue craft available, avoid tides and currents, and have clearly visible buoys. Involve a surf lifesaving club in the organisation of the swim.

The distance can be anywhere up to 800 metres but preferably no more than 500 metres as only the more competent swimmer is able to cover a greater distance comfortably. If the water temperature is below 16°C, shorten the distance so that the participants are not in the water for more than 10 minutes. If the water temperature is below 14°C, cancel the swim!

Every child should wear a brightly coloured bathing cap to prevent heat loss and for easy recognition and always instruct children how to attract attention if they are in trouble. A shallow course which enables the child to stand and rest is ideal, but may be hard to find. Place the children at the start according to their swimming ability to avoid congestion, and instruct officials on symptoms of cold exposure. Facilities should be provided to deal with cases of hypothermia.

cycle

The younger child (8-12) will be able to cycle a distance of 1-4 km comfortably. The course should be traffic free (e.g., school grounds) and simple; either a single loop or an "out back" course as multiple loops are too confusing. The children should be within visible distance of officials.

The distance for the secondary school student can be up to 20 km. The course should be in a low traffic area, avoiding intersections and too many driveways. The course should be one that is easily followed by a child who has never seen the route before.

Helmets are mandatory. No excuses.

Participants should be encouraged to carry a waterbottle on the bike, especially on hot days. An undulating course is more challenging but steep hills should be avoided.

Helmets are mandatory. No excuses.

run
For the primary school child a distance of between 100-2000 metres is appropriate; 12-17 years old can run 5 km. The course should be simple and as safe as it is for the cycle. This is the last event and the most participants will have started to get tired. Aid stations should be available every kilometre and officials should be able to recognise signs of heat illness. Plan the race early in the morning and/or over a shaded course if hot weather is expected.

transition
Clearly mark the transition area and limit entry to participants, volunteers and officials only. Keep parents out of this area. Bike racks make the transition tidier and provide for equality for all participants. The places in the bike rack can either be allocated on a first come, first serve basis or by numbering.

Organised triathlon events are educational for children in that they create a valuable opportunity to teach the participants about proper warming up, pacing, transition strategies and fluid intake.

prizes
The emphasis for children in triathlons should be on encouraging the child to participate in regular aerobic activities for many years to come. T-shirts, medals or certificates for all finishers will help to achieve this. As excellence should be encouraged as well, special prizes should be awarded to top male and female finishers, especially in the 12-17 age group.

conclusion

Triathlons are safe as long as the special needs of the growing child are taken into consideration. Children are maturing and are unique in their physiological and psychological characteristics. They are well suited to submaximal (aerobic) exercise but they do not cope well with extremes in environmental temperature changes. They have a lower motor-efficiency than adults but they perceive exercise as less tiring and recover more quickly from strenuous exercise.

When organising races, distances shorter than the standard triathlon are required and the course needs to be safe as well as easy to follow. Special precautions need to be taken when the temperatures of water and air are extreme.

In the younger age group, the emphasis should be on participation rather than on winning.

The nature of the triathlon allows the child to do most of the training at a comfortable pace so that few risks are involved. The triathlon does not require a high level of skill and is, therefore, an achievable activity. It must be remembered that young children are just as much exposed to the risks of a sedentary lifestyle, stress and poor eating habits as adults. There is an increasing awareness of the importance of health-related fitness events for children as part of prevention of illness-related lifestyle. A combination of swimming, cycling and running exposes the child to an easily accessible and fun way of achieving total body fitness with an improvement in general wellbeing.

about the author

John Hellemans is the holder of six New Zealand triathlon titles, has competed successfully in Australia, Japan, Holland and Hawaii, and at 39 is still representing New Zealand in the elite field. It was under his guidance that Erin Baker exploded onto the international triathlon scene in the mid-1980s, and went on to become the most dominant triathlete, male or female, of the decade, winning numerous world titles in all distances.

While studying medicine John concentrated on the scientific aspects of exercise and performance, including a special research project on metabolism during exercise. He now runs a busy sports medicine practice in Christchurch, and is a convenor of the coaching and medical committees of Triathlon New Zealand.